Archaeology and Her

ARCHAEOLOGY AND HERITAGE

An introduction

John Carman

continuum
LONDON • NEW YORK

Continuum
The Tower Building, 11 York Road, London, SE1 7NX
370 Lexington Avenue, New York, NY 10017-6503

First published 2002 by Continuum by arrangement with the University of Leicester

British Library Cataloguing-in-Publication Data
A catalogue record for this book is available from the British Library.

ISBN 0-8264-5894-7 (hardback)
   0-8264-5895-5 (paperback)

Library of Congress Cataloging-in-Publication Data
Carman, John, 1952–
   Archaeology and heritage: an introduction/John Carman.
     p. cm.
   Includes bibliographical references (p.) and index.
   ISBN 0-8264-5894-7 – ISBN 0-8264-5895-5 (pbk.)
    1. Historic preservation. 2. Material culture—Conservation and restoration.
   3. Antiquities—Collection and preservation. 4. Historic sites—Conservation and restoration.
   5. Archaeology—Methodology. 6. Archaeology—Philosophy. 7. Cultural
property—Protection. 8. Cultural policy. I. Title.

   CC135 .C35 2002
   930.1—dc21   2001047725

Typeset by BookEns Ltd, Royston, Herts
Printed and bound in Great Britain by Bookcraft, Midsomer Norton, Bath

Contents

Preface
The Aims of This Book

This book is intended as an approachable introduction to themes in the field of 'heritage' as it relates to the material legacy of our pasts. It is also intended as an introduction to – and an invitation to indulge in – a way of thinking about issues which are central to the heritage field itself and, indeed, to the interpretation of our pasts. In concentrating upon themes and issues, the book is expressly theoretical in tone: it is not intended as a guide for practitioners on how to 'do' heritage nor does it recommend particular ways of managing the heritage. Nor yet should it be considered as an examination 'primer'. Rather than offering representative examples of heritage practices, it considers such practices in terms of the meanings they hold and the consequences they produce. The book therefore draws upon some current approaches to theorizing material culture and archaeological practice to present to readers some ideas about how we understand and relate to the remains, sites, structures and buildings that have come into our present from the past.

The book is aimed particularly at students of archaeology, history or museum and heritage studies at undergraduate and postgraduate level. It may prove of use to part-time and continuing education students and to those following more advanced studies who find a need to engage with heritage issues. Although designed as a work-text for students, it will also hopefully provide a useful introduction for the more general reader with an interest in archaeology and the material heritage.

Coming to heritage out of archaeology, the book has a deliberately archaeological slant, which may be different from that taken by those who come to heritage out of social history or other related fields. You may also expect it to be very different from those who approach heritage as a branch of leisure, tourist or environmental studies. While there is some affinity – perhaps inevitably – to museum studies, there will be some significant differences from that field too. By 'archaeology' is meant the study of the material remains of the human past, from the most ancient to the most recent. It focuses on material remains, which means those with some physical presence in the world, and does not include the study of the past through texts, or at least not exclusively. 'Material remains' are not limited here to buried objects and features but include also standing monuments and buildings of all types, whether presently in use or not. The term includes objects in museums, in private hands and those not yet discovered. More on definitions will be found in Chapter 1 and throughout the book. All told, the seven chapters are designed to cover the main areas of heritage, which is an area of increasing importance in our world, and a complex and wide one too. The *core* issue – common to all of what the book has to say – is the notion of the relationship between the interpreter of the past (the historian or archaeologist) and the wider world. The latter can be called 'the public' for the moment; although in Chapter 4 it will become evident why the concept of 'the public' is not an easy or simple one to understand or apply.

The overriding themes of the book are twofold. The first is that the heritage is a product of a process best described as 'categorization': the ability to place particular things in certain conceptual boxes, separating them out from all other things in the world and consequently thinking about and treating them differently from the other things in the world. What is called 'the heritage' is just one such conceptual box. The heritage is thus as much a human artefact as any of the individual things that comprise it. The second theme concerns the purpose of the heritage: what we create heritages for and what we can then do with them. Any number of possible purposes spring to mind, but only one is perhaps valid. That is, that any heritage or heritages we create should enhance our understanding of who we are and what we do, and increase our enjoyment and delight in the world we jointly inhabit. If it serves to separate us from that wider environment – by seeking to mark us out as 'special' or 'different' or 'superior', or indeed as 'inferior' – then it is failing in its purpose. Heritages are always 'ours': it is not exclusively mine, nor exclusively yours; like our combined histories, it is something we have in common and which we share with all others. Failure to share the heritage – and thereby ourselves – is to deny the heritage its purpose.

As a work-text the book is divided into seven substantive chapters. These are preceded by a short interlude which considers the types of literature and ways of talking about heritage generally encountered in the field; it also provides a brief introduction to current trends in archaeological theory for those not already well acquainted with the field. Each substantive chapter is divided into a number of key points, indicated by sub-headings. Each of these is reiterated as 'Summary Points' at the end of each chapter and at the end of this section there is also a list of suggested further reading. The texts cited are those which have – one way or another – inspired the thoughts presented in the chapter. The specific content of the book derives from lectures given over a number of years to students of various institutions, among them Cambridge, York, Leicester and Göteborg Universities, and also from papers delivered to audiences at conferences in Italy, Latvia, Portugal, Spain, the UK, the USA and South Africa.

Acknowledgements

I am grateful to all of those who have read and heard what I have had to say over past years, and especially for the kind manner in which it has generally been received. Students have always been keen critics of my ideas, and I am always glad to have their reactions. Of these, I must thank in particular Carol McDavid, Darrin Lee Long and most recently Mary-Catherine Garden for inspiring the thoughts which led to this book and to Carol and Darrin especially for urging the need for such a book when I first mentioned the idea to them. Patricia Carman, Mary-Catherine Garden and Carol McDavid were especially kind to spend time reading the text of chapters as they came out of the printer, and their insightful comments were very useful in shaping the final version you see before you. I also owe to Mary-Catherine, Carol and Laurajane Smith great thanks for responding with speed and grace to my sudden urgent appeal for the reference details of texts I knew existed but unexpectedly found I could not track down.

As always, many friends and colleagues worldwide in what I dare to call (but they may not) 'the heritage field' have made more of a contribution than either they or I can recognize. Among them are Neil Brodie, Martin Carver, Kate Clark, Henry Cleere, Tim Darvill, Chris Evans and the members of the Cambridge Archaeological Unit, Jane Grenville, Graham Fairclough, John Goldsmith, Simon Kaner, Gavin Lucas, Susan Pearce, Professor Lord Renfrew of Kaimsthorn, Tim Reynolds, John Schofield, Laurajane Smith, Marie Louise Stig Sørensen and Elizabeth Stazicker, all based in the UK; Willem Wllems in Holland; Kristian Kristiansen in Sweden; Zbigniew Kobylinski and Wojciech Brzezinski in

Poland; Clay Mathers and Tom Wheaton in the USA; Garry Carnegie, Brian Egloff and Peter Wolnizer in Australia; George Abungu in Kenya; Alinah Segobye in Botswana; Donald Chikumbi and Dennis Haambote in Zambia; Paul Mupira and Joseph Muringaniza in Zimbabwe; and Koji Mizoguchi in Japan. All of these individuals have over the years contributed to the way of approaching heritage offered here: and whether they agree or disagree with specific statements in the book, I hope they are each able to recognise their part in its making. To all of these people I owe much gratitude and friendship, but of course they are not to be held responsible for any errors of fact, infelicities of style or misrepresentations to be found here, which are entirely mine. The Department of Archaeology, University of Cambridge provided the space and working tools to put the book together, and I owe thanks to Jane Woods, Chrissie Spriggs and Vanessa Cole Arthur for their forebearance while I cluttered up the Departmental Office printer with vast amounts of text.

Finally, and as always, the greatest debt goes to my wife Patricia. Without her urging I probably would never have actually started to write this book, merely talked about writing it.

John Carman
Cambridge, July 2001

To Margaret and Richard Carman,
my parents,
who taught me to appreciate the past but also to question it

Introductory Interlude
A Note about Literature and Discourses of Heritage and Archaeology

One of the themes that will emerge in this book is that of the ways in which issues in the heritage field are discussed, who does the talking, and the largely unspoken 'rules' that govern what can be said, about what and by whom. All of these fall under the heading of 'discourse' – a word that will appear quite often in the text. Discourse is concerned with

> all the conditions required for the production of knowledge ... [and is] the structured conditions within which statements can be made ... arranged according to systems and criteria of inclusion and exclusion [including] patterns of authority (committees and hierarchies, for example) and systems of sanctioning, accreditation, and legitimation (degrees, procedures of reference and refereeing, personal experiences, career paths). (Hodder *et al.*, 1995: 235)

Literature

It is possible to divide the literature of the heritage field into three broad classes: inevitably there are some overlaps and some blurring, but in general the three categories do seem to stand scrutiny. As you read this book and the literature cited here, it is always worthwhile considering what kind of approach to the heritage it represents. It is possible to divide the literature up in a way different from that used here. Nevertheless, and however you choose to categorize what you read, it is always a good idea not to take any text quite at face value, including this one.

Commentary

The first body of work in heritage can be described as *commentary*. Most of it is published in book form. Such texts take a broad approach to the notion of heritage, treating it as a cultural phenomenon. Much of this literature is concerned with defining 'heritage' as something separate from 'history' or the 'real' past. Much of it derives from a position that 'heritage' is a bad thing – or at least inferior to the work of academics and others concerned with a more serious investigation of the past. It treats heritage as the field of popularization of the past. Ultimately it is concerned with the issue of representation, particularly in its rather narrow sense of public presentation through museums and heritage centres. This is all valuable literature and interesting to read. It is committed and insightful. It is also virtually irrelevant to practitioners of heritage management because it has little to tell them about how to do what they do; often it misses its audience amongst them because it is so very critical of their efforts.

EXAMPLES

Peter Fowler, *The Past in Contemporary Society: Then, Now* (1992) (international)

Robert Hewison, *The Heritage Industry: Britain in a Climate of Decline* (1987) (UK)

Michael Hunter (ed.), *Preserving the Past: The Rise of Heritage in Modern Britain* (1996) (UK)

David Lowenthal, *The Past Is a Foreign Country* (1985) (international)

David Lowenthal, *The Heritage Crusade and the Spoils of History* (1996) (international)

Kevin Walsh, *The Representation of the Past: Museums and Heritage in the Post-modern World* (1992) (UK)

Patrick Wright, *On Living in an Old Country* (1985) (UK)

Guides to practice

The second body of literature concerns the specific day-to-day *practices* of heritage management. This is very much a body of 'how-to' literature, and, as such, very valuable to heritage practitioners. It is the kind of literature encountered in professional and postgraduate education and training in the field. It comprises many of the works to be found on the shelves of professionals. It concerns the procedures and tools of practical heritage management, especially archaeological heritage management. It is about laws, regulation and procedure. Much of it is dull to read. It is limited in its aim, and much of it adopts an anti-theoretical stance because abstract theory is held to be of little practical relevance. It is very important in the field because it contains so much information on how the field of heritage is perceived by its practitioners. In many ways it represents the typical literature of heritage worldwide; and it is the most widely read and the most seriously treated by practitioners.

EXAMPLES

Martin Carver, 'On archaeological value', in *Antiquity* (1996) (UK)

Henry Cleere (ed.), *Approaches to the Archaeological Heritage* (1984) (international)

Henry Cleere (ed.), *Archaeological Heritage Management in the Modern World* (1989) (international)

Timothy Darvill *et al.*, 'A question of national importance', in *Antiquity* (1987) (UK)

Timothy Darvill *et al.*, 'Identifying and protecting historic landscapes', in *Antiquity* (1993) (UK)

Jeanette Greenfield, *The Return of Cultural Treasures* (1989) (international)

John Hunter and Ian Ralston (eds), *Archaeological Resource Management in the UK* (1993) (UK)

Charles McGimsey, *Public Archaeology* (1972) (USA)

John Pugh-Smith and John Samuels, *Archaeology in Law* (1996) (UK)

Michael Schiffer and George Gumerman (eds), *Conservation Archaeology* (1977) (USA)

Research

The third body of literature – still relatively small, but growing – *researches* the practices of heritage to see what it is that heritage practices themselves produce. These works are not 'commentary' in the sense used earlier because the understandings of what heritage practitioners achieve is not derived from a set of *a priori* assumptions about how the world works, but from actually looking to see how heritage management itself works in the world. It is not procedural – although much of the specific content relates to procedural matters – because it is not intended as a guide to how to do heritage; rather it is about what happens when heritage management is done. That is its value: it is capable of informing heritage practitioners and others what the fruits of their work actually are; not what they should be; nor what they think they are or should be. Whereas so much of the discourse of heritage is about the simplification of complexity, this research is concerned to restore the complexity, but meaningfully and usefully. It represents approaches similar to those which inform this book.

EXAMPLES

Frederick Briuer and Clay Mathers, *Annotated Bibliography on Significance* (1996) (US)

John Carman, *Valuing Ancient Things: Archaeology and Law* (1996) (UK)

Nick Merriman, *Beyond the Glass Case: The Public, Museums and Heritage in Britain* (1991) (UK)

Susan Pearce, *On Collecting* (1995) (UK)

Laurajane Smith, 'Towards a theoretical framework for archaeological heritage management', in *Archaeological Review from Cambridge* (1993) (Australia)

Laurajane Smith, 'Significance concepts in Australian management archaeology' in *Tempus* (1996) (Australia)

Discourses

Heritage

The discourse of heritage in English is also the international discourse, whether in the form of commentary, procedure or research. While the specifics of heritage practice vary from one territory to another – and indeed the name by which it is called (archaeological heritage management [Europe], archaeological resource management [UK], cultural heritage management [Australia], cultural resource management [USA] or public archaeology [USA]) will also vary – the underlying themes and operational practices are the same virtually everywhere. They have been adopted throughout the globe – in Europe, North America, Australia, Oceania, Africa and, increasingly, in Latin America. Recent efforts to introduce 'modern' heritage practices in Korea and Japan are of exactly the same kind. The anglophone international discourse of heritage is thus very powerful.

This discourse – especially as reflected in the literature – can take one of two main forms. As description it can inform as to the way heritage is done and the consequences of doing heritage in that particular way. Whether as commentary, procedure or the products of research, this descriptive discourse tells us how heritage is done and the effects of doing it. The other main style of discourse is informed by an idea of what heritage is for and, therefore, what practitioners should aim to achieve. It is primarily not about what heritage *is*, but about what it *ought* to be. These two discourses are very different and it is dangerous and limiting to confuse them. So much of the literature of heritage is written in the language of *ought* but purports to be in the language of *is*. Thus, Merriman writes at the opening of his book which was the result of the first-ever wide-ranging survey of British public opinion into the past:

> The premise of this book is that the past is something that belongs to all
> ... [The role of museums and similar organizations] as guardians of the
> heritage thus makes them different from other cultural institutions such
> as cinemas, where there is little concern to bring in a public that reflects
> the diversity of the total population. (1991: 1)

Here, Merriman appeals to a shared understanding of the nature of the past, the public, museums and cinemas. The issue here is not whether one agrees with him or not, but that as worded his statement presents that understanding as a set of facts rather than a negotiated agreement subject to other, unstated assumptions. As such, it is an example of the language of *ought* disguised as a statement of what *is*. Statements concerning the nature of heritage or its ownership are frequently of this kind, and all writers on heritage issues are prone to making them. Elsewhere, they masquerade as what I have called 'weasel expressions', that is terms used 'not to clarify but as a well-worn cliché no one bothers to define any more, a form of in-group cipher' (Carman, 1995: 98). Expressions such as 'the public', 'the past' and indeed 'heritage' itself appear in this guise. It is as well to be alert for them, in this book as in any other.

Archaeological theory

One of the aims of this book is to make a direct and coherent link between discussions of heritage issues and the theoretical perspectives applied in the field of archaeology. It is, therefore, perhaps appropriate to give readers - who may not have a background knowledge of the latter - a short introduction to the main current strands.

In general, archaeologists in the English-speaking world who take an express interest in the theoretical foundations of archaeological work divide currently into one of two 'camps': so-called 'processual' and 'post-processual' or 'interpretive' archaeologists. Proponents of both schemes will agree that an interest in explicit theory in archaeology is crucial to doing good archaeology: all archaeological practice, they will say, is grounded in particular theoretical constructs and it is essential that these be clearly addressed and one's theoretical perspective made clear. There are others who feel that such an overt concern with theory is unnecessary and distracting from the business of doing archaeology: for them, the features, objects and other material remains uncovered by archaeology are self-evident, and 'facts' about the past are clearly distinguishable from non-facts. Those with an interest in theory are not so sure about these things.

Processual archaeology, so called, is conceived as 'anthropological science' rather than history, in which *explanation* of the past is derived from explicit methodologies modelled on the hard sciences which may allow the making of cross-cultural generalizations (Hodder *et al.*, 1995: 3). Accordingly, processualists are concerned with 'the recovery [and] systematic description of material culture in the past' (Clarke, 1968: 10) and thereby seek to discover 'general principles of human behaviour *vis-à-vis* materials' (Gould and Schiffer, 1981: xvi). There is a strong emphasis on the archaeologist as a scientist (although not necessarily with a white coat) (Binford, 1977: 1–2). Recent trends represent a focus on the archaeological record as the source of patterned regularities (Hodder *et al.*, 1995: 3; and see below) and attempt to find more sophisticated means for the construction of schemes of social evolution (Yoffee and Sherratt, 1993).

Post-processual or *interpretive* archaeology represents a more recent reaction to the 'hard-science' approach of processualism. Focusing on *understanding* the past (as opposed to explaining it) (Hodder *et al.*, 1995: 5) reforges the connection between archaeology and history (Hodder *et al.*, 1995: 141–78; Barrett, 1995). At the same time, an emphasis is placed upon archaeology as a contemporary practice – which raises questions regarding the politics and morality of archaeology (Hodder *et al.*, 1995: 5). Post-processualism 'attempts to capture a new openness to debate in archaeology ... At the same time, the aim is to ... contribute an independent voice to both intellectual and public debates' (Hodder, 1986: 171) and to encourage multivocality (Hodder *et al.*, 1995: 5). Claims that post-processualism was a 'broad church' encompassing 'a variety of influences including Marxism, structuralism, idealism, feminist critiques and public archaeology' (Hodder, 1986: 171) have been met by criticisms that this strand of archaeological thought does not do what it claims: that it does not challenge the structures of power in the academy, that it fails to address Marxist and feminist critiques and either takes no account of public archaeology in the form of archaeological heritage management (Carman, 1993; Smith, 1994, 2000) or is scathing of it (Shanks and Tilley, 1987: 24–5, 93–4). Instead, some kind of accommodation has been sought between processualism and post-processualism: the emergence of 'cognitive processualism' (Renfrew and Zubrow, 1994) imports the post-processual concern with the symbolic into the processual scheme; while 'interpretive archaeology' seeks to emphasize the areas of common concern between post-processualists and processualists in terms of archaeological practice (Hodder *et al.*, 1995).

The position of this book

In terms of the literature it belongs to, although informed by research into the field, this book is not itself the product of research. Nor, as set out in the Preface, is it a text designed to provide guidance for practitioners. Accordingly, it most closely resembles – like other texts of this kind – a *commentary* upon aspects of heritage as they relate to archaeological theory and practice. Where it differs from other texts of this category is in the approach it takes to heritage, treating it neither as a deficient form of historical study nor as an area parasitic upon such study. Instead, heritage is treated here as a legitimate set of practices which are integral to and parallel with the academic study of the past through material remains. In terms of discourse it attempts to maintain itself within the discourse of *is* and tries not to shift into a discourse of *ought*: how successful I am in achieving this I shall leave the reader to decide.

The approach taken here is broadly post-structuralist (one of the strands of post-processualism: Bapty and Yates, 1990) in the sense that it follows from the understanding that nothing is understood by virtue of itself: instead, all ideas, concepts, words and things are located in structures of *difference*, which allow us to identify and name things not on the basis of themselves alone, but by virtue of their *not* being something else from which they can be distinguished. In this book, I distinguish between certain categories on the basis of what they are not. This approach locates me – and hence this work – on the 'post-processual' wing of contemporary archaeological thought, and towards the more radical tip of that wing.

'World' heritage sites – familiar images of heritage

Plate I.1 Stones of Stenness, Orkney

Plate I.2 The Parthenon, Athens Acropolis, Greece

Plate I.3 The Tower of London, England

1 Heritage All Around Us

The aim of this chapter is to introduce some of the main themes of the heritage field, especially as they relate to the field of archaeology. Each theme will be returned to in more detail in later chapters, but the aim here is to indicate them and give some idea of how they interact to create the complexity of the phenomenon we so often blithely dismiss as (simply) 'the heritage'. The first and crucial point to grasp about a heritage is that the legacy of the past is all around us. While we may (and indeed often do) think of 'the heritage' as those particular objects separated out as being of 'historical' importance, we should bear in mind that everything that comes to us from the past is part of our historic inheritance.

The complexity of heritage

Heritage is at once global and local. The main heritage sites of the world are known and recognized worldwide, regardless of their location. Thus, Stonehenge, the Great Wall of China, Great Zimbabwe, Uluru (Ayer's Rock) and the Egyptian Pyramids – among others - are classed as 'world heritage sites' and generally considered to belong not to their specific locality alone but to the world at large. Other sites – just as 'historical', even as old and as representative of global histories – are deemed to be merely of local value and may go entirely unremarked even by those who live and work nearby. The fact remains, however, that all global heritage sites are also local. Remove Stonehenge from Salisbury Plain, England, and it ceases to be Stonehenge; similarly the Egyptian

Pyramids cease to be Egyptian if removed from Egypt; and the air of mystery around Uluru would be lost if it were transported away from the interior of the Australian continent.

Heritage is therefore not only something that is present in the world. To be 'heritage' it needs also to be noticed as such. What we think of as the heritage largely depends upon the kind of people we are and the circumstances under which we work. Table 1.1 lists various terms used for the components of the archaeological heritage.

The object of enquiry

The term 'archaeological record' has been most commonly applied to the object of archaeological enquiry by researchers. Patrik's useful review of the term's use up to the mid-1980s shows the wide range of meanings the term has had, revealing 'no working consensus on what the term really means and no explicit definition

Table 1.1 Terms for the object of archaeology

The archaeological record	
Processual archaeology	*Post-processual/interpretive archaeology*
Record (of)	Evidence for
Artefacts	Material culture
Contexts/specific attributes	Cultural resources
Culturally deposited objects	Locales

The archaeological heritage	
Archaeologists	*Lawyers*
Heritage	Cultural property
Resource(s)	Cultural object(s)
Cultural resource(s)	Cultural heritage
	Cultural relics
	Cultural treasures
	Cultural goods
	Dealers
	Antiquities
	Antiques

of it as a theoretical concept' (Patrik, 1985: 31). She goes on to resolve the concept into two so-called alternative 'models': a physical model representing processual approaches, interpreted in terms similar to those of a fossilized record; and a textual model representing post-processual approaches, in which the record is held to encode meanings. The differences in approach implied by these different understandings of the record 'cannot be over-emphasized' and are impossible to reconcile or synthesize (Patrik, 1985: 55). Accordingly, she recommends the use of one for understanding fragmentary material remains as found in the ground, and the other for their interpretation in past use (Patrik, 1985: 56). In answer, Hodder has reinterpreted Patrik to suggest that the record contains simultaneously 'two types of meaning' (Hodder, 1986: 171), while Barrett (1987) has gone so far as to challenge the idea of the 'record' altogether. Barrett charges the treatment of archaeological material as a record with an overriding preoccupation with issues of methodology (Barrett, 1987: 5). Instead, he suggests, we need to consider whether 'archaeological evidence' (as he calls it) actually constitutes a record *of* anything at all: 'we should treat [archaeological evidence] not as a *record of* past events and processes but as *evidence for* particular social practices' (Barrett, 1987: 6).

At the gross scale, therefore, archaeological remains as an object of enquiry can constitute a record of something, or evidence for something – that something being located in the past. Individual researchers, however, may also apply other terms to what they consider they deal with. Patrik lists four different contents of the record: material deposits; material remains; archaeological samples; and archaeological reports (Patrik, 1985: 29). For Binford, archaeologists study 'simply artefacts [defined as] all those modifications of natural materials ... that humans ... produce as a result of their lifeways' (Binford, 1989: 3); and Clarke concurred, adding 'the information observed about their contextual and specific attributes' (Clarke, 1968: 13). For Schiffer, the record 'contains culturally deposited objects that [crucially for him] are no longer part of an ongoing society' (Schiffer, 1987: 3). These three represent proponents of Patrik's 'physical' model of the record: for them, the record *as a record of something* exists as a physical fact.

Proponents of the alternatives take a markedly different line. Hodder also studies artefacts (Hodder, 1982: 18) which he designates as 'material culture', a term reinterpreted more abstractly to incorporate the 'meanings [carried by artefacts] through being associated with practical uses in specific contexts' (Hodder, 1989: 72–3). Tilley takes this idea further to cite his concern with material culture as 'a contextualised social act ... a framing and constitutive medium ... a social production' (Tilley, 1989b: 188–9). Tilley also challenges the idea that what he studies is to do with the past: 'The interpretation of meaning and significance of material culture is a contemporary activity. The meaning of the past does not reside in the past but belongs in the present' (Tilley, 1989b: 192). Barrett, by contrast with these, is concerned with what he calls 'cultural resources' being 'a complex series of *locales* within which meaningful and authoritative forms of discourse can be sustained' (Barrett, 1987: 6). For the post-processualist, the record is not a given fact, but is actively created during the course of archaeological practice (Hodder *et al.*, 1995: 12). For Tilley, excavations – far from simply revealing raw data – are 'nexuses of decoding and encoding processes by which' meaning is created (Tilley, 1989a: 280). For Barrett, 'the physical relationships between things ... are data without historical meaning' and consequently 'archaeological practice [should] operate as *historical enquiry*, and not simply the description of contemporary residues' (Barrett, 1995: 9).

The object of management

Those concerned with the management and preservation of ancient material have a different set of terms for the object of their endeavours from researchers. The three most common terms among archaeologists working in this area are: 'the archaeological heritage' (Cleere, 1984a, 1989), the 'archaeological resource' or 'resources' (Darvill, 1987; McGimsey and Davis, 1977); and – especially outside Europe, where the 'prehistoric' record is that of an extant indigenous population – 'cultural resources' (Lipe, 1984).

Table 1.2 Some definitions of the archaeological heritage

- [that which is] governed by legislation (Cleere, 1989)
- all remains ... from past epochs which can illustrate the history of mankind (ICAHM)
- monuments, sites, artefacts, research traditions, knowledge for survival (Trotzig, 1993)
- remains of a *nation's* past (Daniel and Renfrew, 1988)
- sites and monuments (excluding buildings and art works) (Reichstein, 1984)
- *identified* sites (Darvill, 1987)
- physical evidence left on a landscape (Scovill *et al.*, 1977)
- all evidence of past lifeways (McGimsey and Davies, 1977)
- things preserved by legislation (Lipe, 1984)
- containers of information (Fowler, 1982)

The heritage is frequently defined in legal terms: for Cleere it is 'governed by legislation' (Cleere, 1989: 10); for the International Committee for Archaeological Heritage Management it consists of ' "all remains and objects and any other traces of mankind from past epochs" which can illustrate the history of mankind and its relation to the natural environment' on land or under water (Trotzig, 1993: 414). However, the heritage need not consist only of material remains: to monuments, sites and artefacts Trotzig (1987) adds 'research tradition' and 'knowledge for [human] survival'. Trotzig's universality can be replaced with a more specific concern, so that the remains of a particular *nation's* past can be considered part of its heritage (Daniel and Renfrew, 1988: 194) and as a consequence fall prey to the criticisms of the contemporary combination of 'Enterprise and Heritage' as insular and retrospectively nostalgic (Robins, 1991; Walsh, 1992). Alternatively, the management of the archaeological heritage can be limited to 'archaeological sites and monuments' while a separate field of architectural and artistic resource management 'covers historic buildings and works of art' (Reichstein, 1984: 37).

The archaeological resource 'applies to all *identified* sites' (Darvill, 1987: 25, emphasis added), may '*predominately* consist of the physical evidences ... left on a landscape by past societies'

(Scovill *et al.*, 1977: 45, emphasis added) or can be extended to '*all* evidences of past human occupation which can be used to reconstruct the lifeways of past peoples' (McGimsey and Davis, 1977, 109, emphasis added). Cultural resources include 'things preserved by legislation' (Lipe, 1984, 3) and 'may be thought of as "containers" of information, or potential information, about past human activities' (Fowler, 1982: 19). This latter understanding is very similar to that of Barrett (1987), although it is important to bear in mind that Barrett is himself critical of archaeological heritage management practice.

As something governed by or things preserved under law (Cleere, 1989: 10), heritage can be considered as quite a narrow range of objects: if it is not subject to treatment by law, and especially if not preserved under that law, then it is not heritage. As the 'remains of a nation's past', things representing global, ethnic or regional, local or family pasts will be excluded from inclusion in the heritage: these ideas will be revisited in Chapter 7. Similarly, if only 'identified sites' are included, then things which are not sites are excluded; and so are those sites not yet identified. As 'sites and monuments' only, the heritage excludes standing buildings and art works along with anything else not considered to be either a site or a monument. As 'physical evidence left on' (but not in) a landscape, it excludes both non-physical evidence and that not left on a landscape. 'All evidence from past epochs' sounds like a fairly inclusive definition, except that it covers only that relating to the history of mankind, which immediately raises the issue of the histories of other humans including women and children, and is also limited to that *illustrating* history: evidence that does less, or conceivably more, is thus left out of this definition of the archaeological heritage; and nothing modern or contemporary with our own age is included. A definition that covers not only sites, monuments and artefacts but also forms of knowledge is perhaps the most inclusive, but only certain forms of knowledge are included, suggesting that there may be some left out of account. A definition that includes 'all evidences for past lifeways' is also limited to the past, but may be stretched to include the near-present and there is no limitation placed upon the types of evidence, which takes us inevitably beyond archaeology, which may not be such a bad thing. The final definition – of heritage as 'a container of information' – does not specify which kinds of information nor how it is held, and will need to be used in conjunction with one of the other more limiting definitions to make it usable.

These definitions are all taken from the literature of archaeological heritage management and accordingly at least one major writer in the field lays claim to each of them. The treatment of them here is deliberately – and probably unfairly – harsh, but is done to illustrate the problem inherent in attempting to define what we mean by 'heritage'. The problem is inevitably worse as one moves beyond the discipline of archaeology alone: and yet 'heritage' is clearly an interdisciplinary concept. Each definition includes certain kinds of things but excludes others. This double action – of inclusion and simultaneous exclusion – is a direct product of the categorization process that lies at the heart of heritage.

Alternative forms

It is clear from this brief review of archaeological terminology that opinions differ among researchers into the human past as to the nature of the phenomenon with which they have to deal, although by and large they apply the same term to it. By contrast, those concerned with the preservation and management of archaeological material use a range of different terms which by and large refer to the same set of understandings.

Here, we are concerned to gauge some sense of the differences between the archaeological *record* – the object of investigation – and the archaeological *resource* or *heritage* – the object of management and preservation. It is always important to grasp that the material constituting the record, the resource and the heritage is identical – it is the full range of material with which all archaeologists deal. The differences between the concepts can be seen as a series of transformations along various 'dimensions' applicable to both: Table 1.3 summarizes these transformations.

These phenomena are of concern to two different groups of people. As 'record' or a 'resource', archaeological material is primarily of concern to field archaeologists researching into the past. As 'heritage', however, it is primarily considered to be of

Table 1.3 Archaeological objects: measures of difference between the archaeological *record,* the archaeological *resource* and the archaeological *heritage*

Criterion	The Archaeological ...		
	Record	**Resource**	**Heritage**
Of concern to	archaeologists	archaeologists	the public
Key attribute	variability	finite/non-renewable	representativeness
Used for	research	preservation for research	preservation for access
Creation of	archaeological theory/method	regulation	regulation
Considered as	evidence	resource	source
Identified by	survey	categorization	categorization
Selected for	relevance	significance	importance
Concerns (time)	past	present	present

Direction of travel ⟶
of material from record to heritage.

But this is also a *realm of transformation* from one type of archaeological object to another because all these categories are made of the same material. ⟵⟶

concern to the public (McGimsey, 1972: 5; Fowler, 1984; Merriman, 1991). The diagnostic attribute of the record is that of variability: for Binford it takes the form of variability in assemblages of artefacts, in form, in function and in style (Binford, 1983); for Hodder it takes the form of temporal, spatial, depositional and typological variability (Hodder, 1986: 125). The diagnostic attributes of the resource, however, are that it is finite and consequently non-renewable (Darvill, 1987: 1; McGimsey, 1972: 24). As heritage, the key attribute it must possess is representativeness of a period of the past or a class of material (Cleere, 1984c: 127). The use to which the record will be put is always that of research, whereas the resource and the heritage will be preserved, the one for future research, the other for public access. In fulfilling its research role, the record and the resource both constitute evidence to be used in understanding the past, the one immediately and the other in the future (Barrett, 1987: 6). By contrast, the heritage constitutes a resource for creating and sustaining a sense of cultural identity in the present (Lipe, 1984: 2; Fowler, 1992; Darvill, 1987: 4). In seeking the record, various techniques of survey are applied (Cleere, 1984c: 126) while the resource and heritage are subject to characterization studies and processes of categorization (Darvill, 1993; Carman, 1996c). Once identified, components of the record are selected for use on the basis of their relevance to specific research projects (Binford, 1977: 2), whereas components of the resource and heritage are selected on the basis of their ascribed significance or importance (Cleere, 1984c: 127; Schaafsma, 1989; Wester, 1990). Overall, the record relates in general to the past: for Patrik (1985: 56), the 'physical' model relates to the condition of the record in the present, while the 'textual' model relates to the use of whole objects in the past; Binford's claim to study 'artefacts' (Binford, 1989: 3) may cover both. By contrast, the resource and the heritage are *always* a phenomenon of the present.

Since these three phenomena represent different 'versions' of the same body of material, they are capable of transformation from one to another, back and forth. Indeed, the creation of the heritage as a category is little more than a process of the designation and changes in accepted treatment of particular kinds of material. This is frequently represented in archaeology by the sequence record – resource – heritage, which also represents the normal 'direction of travel' of a body of archaeological material from discovery onwards (cf. Schiffer, 1972; Carman, 1990). On first discovery, archaeological remains are part of the archaeological record and are considered and treated as such. Once discovered, however, they may also become part of the archaeological resource, to be kept for the future benefit of archaeology as a discipline. At a subsequent stage this material may be considered as appropriate for a more public audience, and will become part of the heritage that is of concern to the community as a whole. This trajectory from record through resource to heritage is normal because rarely – if indeed ever – will something be classed as 'heritage' on immediate discovery and subsequently transformed to 'mere' record. This trajectory therefore represents not only a change in designation and treatment but also a change in valuation, to be discussed further in Chapter 6.

Archaeologists and lawyers

The archaeological record is the domain of archaeological theory and methodology (Patrik, 1985), while the archaeological resource and the archaeological heritage are very largely that of law (Cleere, 1989: 10; McGimsey, 1972; McGimsey and Davis, 1977: 9; Fowler, 1982: 4–12; Schiffer and Gumerman, 1977: 3–7). For official purposes, the archaeological resource consists only of those things defined and identified by law.

Table 1.4 The heritage in England (1 and 2) and the USA (3)

---

1. *The archaeological heritage in England*

Ancient monuments
Land of scenic, historic or scientific interest
Treasure Trove items
Conservation areas
National nature reserves
Sites of special scientific interest
Areas of outstanding natural beauty
National parks
Military remains
Environmentally sensitive areas

Source: Darvill, 1987: 32–9

---

2. *The architectural and historic heritage in England*

Scheduled ancient monuments
County records of sites and monuments
Listed buildings
Conservation areas
Historic parks and gardens

Source: Somerset County Council 1989

3. *The historic heritage in the USA*

Historic properties
Historic sites, buildings and objects of national significance
Archaeological resources, including pottery, basketry, bottles, weapon projectiles, tools, structures or portions of structures, pit houses, rock paintings, rock carvings, intaglios, graves, human skeletal materials ... at least 100 years of age
Shipwrecks

Source: US Department of the Interior 1989–90

Two things are evident from the summary contained in Table 1.4. First, that such legal descriptions vary according to jurisdiction: not only are the terms different in England and the USA, but also in the national and county levels within England. Second, it is evident that in all cases the material described carries a significant burden of pre-valuation as 'ancient', 'historic', or 'archaeological'; this is inevitable since it represents those things that have already been accepted by the legal process as worthy of preservation. Indeed, the ultimate purpose of law in this area is to provide a value for such material (Carman, 1996c). In general, however, lawyers do not apply the same terminology as archaeologists to ancient remains.

Greenfield (1989, 225–55) usefully reviews the use and meaning of the terms 'cultural property', 'cultural object', 'cultural heritage', 'cultural relic' and 'cultural treasure'. While O'Keefe and Prott (1984) declared an early preference for the term 'relic', Greenfield prefers 'cultural treasure', and Palmer and his associates prefer 'cultural property' for the titles of their legally and economically inclined journals. Differences in the choice of term relate to the intention behind the choice. Geenfield seeks to separate out cultural *treasures* as constituting 'only exceptional or unique landmark objects' (Greenfield, 1989: 255) because she seeks to determine legal criteria for the return of such objects to their original location; she accepts that such return can only ever be exceptional, and so only applies to exceptional items. O'Keefe and Prott (1984) are concerned to record the coverage of law of all components of the archaeological heritage and thus seek a term for individual items that is as wide and (relatively) value-free as possible: for them, 'relic' is a term descriptive of the physical form of an item, not a value ascription; their more recent declaration is for 'cultural heritage' as one encompassing the concerns of all interests (O'Keefe and Prott, 1992). Greenfield concentrates her discussion on the notion of the object as representative of 'culture'. She focuses in particular on the broad usage of the term, comprising as it does 'both the *Mona Lisa* and a photograph of the living room of a French steelworker' (Greenfield, 1989: 252) and citing with ironic disdain O'Keefe and Prott's (1984: 33) extension of the concept of 'cultural heritage' to include human faeces (Greenfield, 1989: 255); from a strictly archaeological perspective, however, such remains can be of immense value in understanding the past.

The reduction of complexity

The preceding discussion shows that the heritage field is something about which little simple agreement exists. Its object has a range of different names depending upon who is concerned with it and for what purpose. It is made up of physical material that can just as easily be classed as something other than heritage – as history, as archaeology, as architecture, as art or, indeed, as nature. It is the result of a process of categorization of which we are only dimly aware and which as effectively excludes as it includes material for our consideration. And yet – despite all this – 'the heritage' as a concept is one with which we are, in general, happy. We know what we mean by it and we think we know what others mean by it, what it is for and how it should be treated. Thus, in much of the literature of heritage, the basic principles upon which those who are responsible for the heritage base their work are deemed to be very few (Table 1.5). What follows from this is that the kinds of treatment to which the heritage is subject are also very few (Table 1.6).

Table 1.5 Basic principles of heritage management

1. The heritage is finite and non-renewable.
2. It is a matter of public concern.
3. It is governed by legislation.
4. It cannot all be preserved and so must be assessed for its value.

Table 1.6 Key practices of heritage management

Inventory
Evaluation
Preservation/Conservation
Rescue archaeology
Presentation

It is a fundamental belief of heritage managers that the quantity of material surviving from the past is finite – that is, there is only so much of it existing – and that it cannot be renewed once it is lost. Any loss of material from the past is thus irrecoverable. Since the past is something owned by us all, it is a matter of public concern that appropriate measures should be taken to ensure that its loss is controlled. Accordingly, laws are passed to regulate the nature and treatment of the heritage, making it subject to governance by legislation: all countries of the world have some legislation relating to their heritage, an issue that will be further addressed in Chapter 3. However, since not all that survives can be preserved forever, it is necessary to select the best and most representative examples for preservation by assessing them for their relative value. The recognized practices of heritage management are grounded upon these four principles.

The first need is to know what exists: hence one of the first things managers of the heritage must do is to carry out surveys to find what is there and record it appropriately. The material must then be evaluated to see whether it is considered worthy of preservation or can be allowed to be lost to development or other processes: appropriate valuation criteria are usually applied for this process. Those selected for preservation will be subject to varying types of control, depending upon local conditions and traditions: they may merely be left alone or may become the object of programmes of restoration and other conservation work. Those not selected for preservation may be allowed to be lost or may instead become subject to programmes of research (in the case of archaeology, often destructive excavation) prior to loss. Preserved sites, monuments and objects may become places which the wider public may visit as preserved items or may be left open as an amenity for enjoyment in other ways. An excavation may similarly allow public access to watch the results as the work progresses.

Heritage themes

Heritage is thus a complex field out of which emerge a few simple principles and internationally recognized standard practices. One reason for this apparent paradox, of a field of complexity that results in simple practices, is that the heritage field is one that works hard to avoid the complexities in which it is enmeshed. To understand heritage, it is necessary to separate elements out and treat them as discrete things. Once we understand them, we believe we understand heritage. What we forget to do is to put them back together to see how they interact. One of the most common approaches is to consider the phenomenon of 'heritage' as a product of another process, such as nationalism or the rise of international capital, without linking this back to other issues in heritage. This serves to simplify, and indeed often to denigrate, the heritage as a phenomenon as in so much of the literature earlier described as 'commentary'. This book will try to take a different approach. Each of the following five chapters will take a theme relevant to the creation or treatment of the heritage and endeavour to open it up to examination and criticism. These themes will then be reconsidered in Chapter 7 under broader themes relating to the heritage, in an effort to show the ways in which heritage themes interact to produce the complex phenomenon of heritage. Among these themes are those listed in Table 1.7.

Table 1.7 Themes in the heritage field

Value
Categories of material
The 'semiotics' of the material world
Aesthetic and emotional responses
Otherness, alienation and commodification
The dissemination of information – including presentation and display
The role of archaeology (and related disciplines) in society

The issue of the values we give to heritage material will be considered in Chapter 6. The categories of material that become part of the heritage will be addressed in Chapter 2. The 'semiotics' of the material ·world – that is, the way meaning is given to things and the kinds of meaning they carry – will appear in several chapters, but will most openly be addressed in Chapter 5. Issues concerning our emotional responses to such material will be addressed in Chapters 5 and 6, while the issues of turning such material into commodities will lie behind much of what is discussed in Chapter 5 along with other issues relating to public display and access. The role of academic disciplines in wider society forms part of the discussion of relations with 'the public' in Chapter 4. All these issues will re-emerge in Chapter 7.

Further reading

Archaeological practice and theory

Hodder, I. (1992) *Reading the Past: Current Approaches to Interpretation in Archaeology*. Cambridge: Cambridge University Press.
Hodder, I., Shanks, M., Alexandri, A., Buchli, V., Carman, J., Last, J. and Lucas, G. (eds) (1995) *Interpreting Archaeology: Finding Meaning in the Past*. London: Routledge.
Hodder, I. and Preucel, R. (1996) *Contemporary Archaeology in Theory: A Reader*. Cambridge, MA: Blackwell.
Johnson, M. (1999) *Archaeological Theory: An Introduction*. Oxford: Blackwell.
Renfrew, C. and Bahn, P. (2000) *Archaeology: Theories, Methods and Practice*, 3rd edn. London: Thames & Hudson.

AHM in archaeology

Brisbane, M. and Wood, J. (1996) *A Future for Our Past? An Introduction to Heritage Studies*. London: English Heritage.
Gould, S. (1998) 'Planning, development and social archaeology', in S. Tarlow and S. West (eds), *The Familiar Past? Archaeologies of Later Historical Britain*. London: Routledge.

Schiffer, M. B. (1979) 'Some impacts of cultural resource management on American archaeology', in J. R. McKinley and R. Jones (eds), *Archaeological Resource Management in Australia and Oceana*. Wellington, NZ: New Zealand Historic Places Trust, 1–11.

Smith, L. (1993) 'Towards a theoretical framework for archaeological heritage management', *Archaeological Review from Cambridge*, **12**(1): 55–75.

Summary points

1. The heritage is all around us, but not necessarily visible to us, because we do not 'see' it as heritage.
2. Heritage is a complex field. There is no common agreement as to what to call the heritage: what you call it depends on how you approach it and what you consider it to be for. There is no commonly accepted definition of what comprises the heritage; any definition at once includes certain types of things while inevitably excluding others.
3. The heritage is created by a process of categorization. It is an artefact in the same way as the objects we call 'heritage'. Anything comprising the heritage can just as easily – and for someone else probably will – be considered as something other than the heritage. In archaeology, the material comprising the heritage is also the record and vice versa.
4. Although a field of great complexity and disagreement, it is one also in which the drive is towards simplification. Heritage is thus often regarded as a realm not of complex ideas but of relatively few practices. This may be one of the reasons for its attraction as a field of study and employment.
5. Nevertheless, the issues of heritage involve very difficult ones: these include such complex ideas as value, meaning, emotional response, commodification and the role of the professional in society.

Heritage objects in the landscape

Plate 1.1 Ruins of Rievaulx Abbey, Yorkshire, England

Plate 1.2 Walls of Byzantium, Istanbul, Turkey

Plate 1.3 Ottoman fortress beside the Bosphorus, Istanbul, Turkey

Plate 1.4 Bronze Age barrows along the skyline, Avebury, Wiltshire, England

Plate 1.5 Tara – the seat of kings – Ireland

2 Components of the Heritage and Their Treatment

The theme of categories was introduced in Chapter 1. This chapter will continue that theme by considering those things out of which the heritage is constructed. The opening section introduces the idea that each material component of the archaeological object is very different from the others. It is therefore an attempt to explain why each must be treated separately. This is not, however, an attempt to define them in absolute terms, to derive an 'essence' which applies in all times and all places. Rather, it is an attempt to locate these categories in modern consciousness, especially in terms of the way archaeologists – and others concerned with the material remains of the past (the 'managers' of 'the heritage') – usually think.

Objects, sites and landscapes

Julian Thomas (1993: 19) has pointed out that landscapes have entered archaeology rather late in its history: they are the third thing to enter the archaeological consciousness after objects became a focus of enquiry, and after monuments and sites which succeeded objects. This movement – from objects to monuments to landscapes – can be read as a simple movement up-scale over time, each phase incorporating a bigger type of object than the one before. This way of thinking in which categories of archaeological material are arranged in hierarchies is the one typically encountered in archaeology.

Darvill and his colleagues attempted to construct a means of classifying and categorizing what they termed 'relict cultural landscapes' and to set about identifying in the real world the types

Table 2.1 Landscapes as containers (1)

Contexts, features, components
Monuments, in groups, clusters and complexes
Patterns and regularities in groups and clusters of monuments
Relict cultural landscapes: single period or multi-period

Source: Darvill *et al.,* 1993

of historically created landscape they had thus described (Darvill *et al.,* 1993). Table 2.1 lists the types of things they say archaeologists are concerned with:

at the lowest level, single contexts, features and components;
above that, monuments to be found grouped, clustered and in complexes;
above that, patterns and regularities in groups and clusters of monuments;
above and containing all these, relict cultural landscapes.

Reading the list in reverse, relict cultural landscapes can be seen to comprise regularities in groups and clusters of monuments, each individual monument then containing single and multiple contexts, features and components. Here is a neat hierarchical structure which derives from and meets archaeological expectation. It is similar to the approach taken elsewhere by Geoffrey Wainwright, who in his paper entitled 'The management of the English landscape' (Wainwright, 1989a) is in fact concerned only with monuments. For those concerned with the preservation and management of historic landscapes, those landscapes are containers: what they contain are monuments.

Table 2.2 Landscapes as containers (2)

Monuments
Artefacts: pottery, flints, metalwork, grave goods
Ecofacts: bone, cereals, C^{14} samples
[Human beings]

Source: Barrett, Bradley and Green, 1991

Table 2.2 is taken from a book entitled *Landscape, Monuments and Society*, which can itself be read as a kind of hierarchy – the landscape containing monuments which are the product of social action, but which the authors say is the sequence in which they progressed from one focus of interest to another (Barrett, Bradley and Green, 1991: 1). Landscapes here are again things that contain other things: some of the things contained are monuments, which in turn contain artefacts such as pottery, flints, metalwork and grave goods, all against a kind of 'background' of ecofacts such as pieces of bone, wood, cereals, charcoals and carbon 14 samples (Barrett, Bradley and Green, 1991: 15–6, Tables 1.1–1.2). But – and here the interest in things *social* comes through – at the same time the landscape is one that human beings – real people – move through: 'A time–space perspective ... is concerned with the routine movement of people through landscapes, constituted by the locales in which they came into contact' (Barrett, Bradley and Green, 1991: 7–8). This is an approach since developed by John Barrett (1994) and Julian Thomas (1991), among others, in which landscapes are understood not only to contain inanimate things such as monuments and objects, but also living, breathing and acting human beings.

This hierarchical approach to looking at archaeological material – in which the highest level phenomena (landscapes) are seen as large containers for smaller things – is typical of archaeologists when they approach landscape archaeology, and much good work has come out of this kind of approach. The two examples contained in Tables 2.1 and 2.2 do *not* represent 'poor' archaeology but, instead, represent some of the best in the fields of archaeological research and resource management. The hierarchical ordering of categories is, however, very interesting, because it does not allow for major disjunctive breaks *between* orders of material: a monument in the hierarchical ordering of phenomena is a big fixed object, objects are treated pretty much as ecofacts are (and vice versa), and landscapes are simply treated as expansive monument clusters and groups. Archaeologists can move conceptually from object to monument to landscape and back without any shift in mental gear, without reorganizing their behaviour or their worldview.

My previous work in the field of archaeological heritage

management has been concerned with the way in which things are categorized; the ways in which archaeologists treat the things placed into those categories; and what this tells us about the value systems in which archaeologists work. In particular, the approach focused on the study of English law and what it has to say about archaeological material, especially in terms of the kinds of values it is given and what one is allowed to do with it. That work established that the values allowed by law resolve into one of two kinds: one of greater *amenity* value, representing something for some kind of use (not necessarily destructive) immediately; or one of greater *scientific* value, representing something to be stored as a source of knowledge to be retrieved in the future. These value types are arranged along a continuum which runs from total amenity value (with little or no scientific component) to total scientific value (with little or no amenity component), but most are mixed in various degrees (Carman, 1996c).

Applying this approach to issues concerning the preservation or rehabilitation of wetland areas, it becomes evident that different value types are operating. Rehabilitators (those who wish to restore wetland areas to some prior condition, in order to encourage particular habitats) are mostly treating wetland sites as current *amenities* – something to be used *now* for current purposes, not necessarily exclusively human (Johnson, 1996). On the other hand, preservationists opposed to rehabilitation (such as archaeologists and palaeoecologists) see wetland sites as sources of *scientific* knowledge, to be retrieved at some unspecified time in the *future*. These different value ascriptions are related to very different sets of expectations concerning and behaviours towards wetlands (Carman, 1996a).

The same principles apply at a broader conceptual level. Table 2.3 shows the types of value English law says can be applied to the categories of object, site and landscape. Objects and sites have been grouped together here for convenience and also because they share some similar types of value ascription: they can be of national importance or of archaeological, artistic or scientific interest. Landscape values can easily be separated, however: landscapes share only two types of value ascription with sites, those of 'public interest' and 'scenic interest'; the rest are different. What is more,

Table 2.3 Values under English law

Value type	Landscapes	Objects/sites
Amenity +		Treasure Trove
		Memorial
	Right of way	
	Recreation	
	Access	
	Picnic	
	Sport	
	Natural beauty	
	Open air	
	Public	Public
	Sensitive	
		Appearance
		Character
	Scenic	Scenic
		Traditional
		Aesthetic
		Artistic
		Architectural
		Archaeological
		Historic
		Historical
	Nature conservation	
	Information	
	Learning	
Scientific +	Research	Scientific

Source: Carman, 1998: 33

on the scale that runs from amenity value to scientific value the types of value relating to landscapes tend to cluster at the *amenity* end of the scale while those relating to sites cluster towards the *scientific* end of the scale, with some overlap in the middle and some different landscape values occupying space at the *scientific* end. This suggests that sites and landscapes are valued in very different ways: landscapes as an amenity for present use; monuments and sites as stores of future knowledge.

Movable objects and sites are distinguished in the way we treat them. In general, whenever the issue of the preservation of a heritage *object* is being considered, the concern is one of *ownership*. This is the issue in Treasure Trove hearings (Hill, 1936) and in the transfer of objects to museums (Palmer, 1991). In the case of archaeological sites or monuments, the issue is one of *controls on use*: the ownership does not change (e.g. scheduling or guardianship arrangements for monuments under UK law) but the owner and others are limited in what they can do to the site or monument; and the same applies in the case of UK planning regulation (Department of the Environment, 1990). Nevertheless, objects and sites or monuments have one characteristic in common: they are discrete entities, clearly separable from what surrounds them, easily demarcated and bounded in the case of individual objects, and relatively so in the case of sites and monuments. Move an object from its present location and it remains itself, whatever it is: a pen, a clock, a door. Sites and monuments cannot be moved without losing some of their identity: the stones of Stonehenge moved to the Lake District would not constitute the site of Stonehenge; but you can mark the boundary of the site of Stonehenge in a way that makes sense to people. Not so the landscape.

Table 2.4 is a preliminary attempt to summarize the ideas discussed here. Each of the three main columns covers a particular category, showing its distinctive characteristics and, at the foot, the

Table 2.4 Objects of heritage: categories defining various types of heritage object

Realm of the discrete		**Realm of the connected**
Object	*Site and monument*	*Landscape*
Mobile, but always remains 'itself': 'solid'	Fixed in space: 'bounded'	Extensive: 'unbounded'; changes over time
Object of property: exclusive ownership	Subject to custodianship: controls on use	Cannot be owned or controlled: a product of modern *gaze* dependent on point of view

value realm appropriate to it, in terms of how it is generally treated. The left-hand column concerns movable objects: no matter where an object is or how long it stays there it remains identifiable as a particular kind of object; and the value realm is that of property, in the sense of ownership. The central column concerns sites and monuments: these are fixed in space and can be distinguished from their surroundings by having boundaries placed around them; the value realm is one of control on use rather than change of ownership. The right-hand column concerns landscapes, which are not single things which can have a boundary placed around them: they are extensive and fill the space between other things. That is why the landscape in particular is something different from other categories of thing. Strictly speaking, it may not constitute a *thing* at all. Objects and sites or monuments are discrete, separable and identifiable single things: the landscape is the set of relationships that gives them their separateness. The conceptual gap between the discrete thing and the landscape is an unbridgeable one: they exist in separate conceptual realms. Here I call these the *realm of the discrete* (for objects and sites and monuments) and the *realm of the connected* (for the landscape). However, what this fundamental difference in our apprehension of these categories also means is that there are clear differences between movable items, fixed sites and monuments and landscapes. Each must be treated separately from the others if these conceptual differences are to be accommodated.

It is worth noting that there are certain categories of thing that do not fit into this tripartite scheme. Among these are environmental and other data (such as chemical residues and carbon-14 dates) which exist at a level below that of the object: they cannot be picked up and carried around nor conveniently identified except as attributes of something else that can usually be defined as some kind of object. Similarly, human remains constitute neither objects as artefacts nor yet something large and fixed enough to be considered a site: humans in our framework of thought are conveniently separated out from all other classes of object in the universe; although the archaeological treatment of human remains has led to both problems and new opportunities, as discussed in Chapter 5. Rock art – an area of increasing interest to archaeologists

(Chippindale and Taçon, 1998) - can be treated as 'art', in which case it is usually ascribed some of the qualities of a movable object, such as a painting. It can also be treated more as a 'site', in which case it is ascribed many of the attributes of a fixed monument. It cannot, however, be both at once. Gardens and certain other areas of land can be treated as having many of the attributes of fixed sites rather than unbounded landscapes. At one level they perhaps ought to be considered as landscapes, but they are usually too bounded by physical or conceptual limits to truly merit membership of this category. Beyond all of these things – and indeed beyond objects, sites and landscapes – is the largest category of all: the 'environment' which contains all these things within it. It is at once too large and too unbounded to be captured in a convenient scheme such as this.

These categories, therefore, must be treated with a certain caution. While each is 'real' in the sense that it is meaningful to us and sufficiently reflective of external reality to merit attention, they are also convenient fictions we use to make sense of the world around us. Here, they are used to provide a convenient structure for a discussion of the kinds of things that can be considered as 'heritage'.

Heritage categories

Portable objects

The portable object has certain characteristics that distinguish it from other heritage objects. It has a physical shape with a recognizable exterior. It is also not rigidly fixed to one particular place: it can be removed and remain recognizably itself wherever it is put.

In general across the world, ancient and historically interesting objects you can pick up and carry around are deemed appropriate not for leaving at the place where they were found nor for inclusion as part of another structure, but for placing in a glass case as part of a collection. This is what we do to such objects: we take them away from where they were found and put them in a special place where we can go and look at them. As such, they are subject to a conventional series of treatments:

- retrieval/discovery;
- (physical) conservation to maintain the fabric;
- collection/curation (involving recording and documentation as part of an institutionalized practice);
- (possible) display;
- (possible) trading.

In general, such objects will follow a path that will lead them either to the status of 'portable antiquity' or to that of 'museum object'. The portable antiquity may find itself part of a privately held and owned collection or be traded in the international market for such objects. The museum object is one held by a particular kind of institution (see Chapter 3) for purposes of public access and education. Both these categories depend upon the recognition of the object as 'genuine' or 'authentic' – both of which are ascribed qualities rather than being inherent in the object. Its age may be a factor in ascribing authenticity to an object, although not all 'old' things are held to be authentic, nor are all 'authentic' things necessarily very old (Gell, 1986: 121; Holtorf and Schadla-Hall, 2000).

Drawing upon such ideas, James Clifford's (1988, 224–6) model of the 'art-culture system' is simply 'a machine for making authenticity'. Objects can be moved around in a four-cornered space between the categories of 'artefact' and 'masterpiece' (one diagonal dimension) and between 'inauthentic' and 'authentic' (the other diagonal). In this space, items can become any one of the following:

> *art*, which is original and singular; this is the realm of connoisseurship, the art museum and the art market;
> *culture*, which is traditional and collective; this is the realm of history and folklore, the ethnography museum, of material culture and its study, and of craft;
> *not-culture*, which is new and uncommon; the realm of fakes, inventions, the museum of technology, the ready-made and so-called 'anti-art'; and
> *not-art*, which is reproduced and commercial; this is the realm of tourist art, commodities, the curio collection and utilities (Clifford, 1988: 224)

ASSEMBLAGES AND COLLECTIONS

Movable objects interact with each other in technical, social and conceptual frames. The technological frame is likely to be a physical structure – holding all the parts of the machine together. The social frame may well also be physical – perhaps a building in which certain types of objects come together. The conceptual frame – physically much more ephemeral – is what determines which types of objects shall come together, where and how. Thus, while all objects carry meaning, none carries it by itself: 'one physical object has no meaning by itself ... The meaning is in the relation between all the goods' (Douglas and Isherwood, 1979: 72). This reflects the same understanding as Schiffer's (1987) 'relational' properties of artefacts from archaeological contexts, and the contextual approach advocated by Hodder (1986). Most sets of artefacts – those where the logic of the association between them is not imposed from the start but has to be sought – constitute assemblages. The collection is something different: it can be thought of either as a special kind of assemblage, in which the association between individual artefacts is imposed from the outset, or as a separate entity entirely.

For Clifford (1988: 218) the collection is a strategy in the Western world 'for the deployment of a possessive self, culture and authenticity'. Accordingly, a good collection is one that has been carefully selected, ordered and classified. The collection creates 'the illusion of adequate representation ... by cutting objects out of the specific context [of use] ... and making them "stand for" abstract holes' in the world of the collector (Clifford, 1988: 220). Pearce (1995) suggests that the themes of collecting in Europe are those of identity and individualism, and of control and ownership. 'Collections are essentially a narrative of [personal] experience' (Pearce, 1995: 412) in which the private 'world of the collection [acts] as [an] extended self' (Pearce, 1995: 176). The collection transforms the objects collected, taking chaos and turning it into sense, ordering time and space, and serving to create relationships for collectors both with others and with themselves. Collecting consists of the 'ascription of name and categories' to things (Pearce, 1995: 181) and is 'a manipulation of scale, the attempt to create a world in miniature in which the collector has ultimate control' (Pearce, 1995: 188).

These themes are identical whether one is concerned with the private collection of an individual or the public collection in the museum. Pearce identifies the relationships between the personal and the communal as those also between: the souvenir and the relic; and the heirloom and the heritage (Pearce, 1995: 319). The latter can be considered as a form of collecting by the corporate group; this 'can make its demand [on resources] in the name of unborn generations. ... Only the group can develop a full-fledged otherworldly morality for the group outlives its individual members' (Douglas and Isherwood, 1979: 37). It is the 'otherworldly morality' of the collective that gives the heritage its special status in modern communities. As the souvenir comes from somewhere other than home, so much of the public collections of Western museums originate from exotic places (Clifford, 1988: 222; Pearce, 1995: 336). This leaves non-Western museums in a quandary: 'African museums may not have any antiques or works of artistic value to fit foreign definition, but African arts and crafts are of intrinsic value which is specifically African' (Mbunwe-Samba, 1989: 116). As always, the collection concerns questions of identity, and in so doing the collection becomes an assemblage of 'sacred things' carefully set aside to constitute 'gifts to the self' (Pearce, 1995: 407): collecting is thus an 'erotic experience' (Pearce, 1995: 408). There has perhaps been a 'long term narrative' of collecting in Europe (Pearce, 1995: 406), traceable from the 'prehistoric origin of European individualism' (Pearce, 1995: 85) to the post-modern era. Throughout, the twin themes of identity and control are evident, whether the type of collection is the 'souvenir', the 'fetishistic' or the 'systematic' (Pearce, 1992: 69–88). In all cases, the object in the collection becomes something special.

LOOTING AND TRADING

There is a vast international trade in antiquities. Much of this is illicit, being a trade in stolen, looted, or illegally exported objects. Each of these classes of objects is 'illicit' but in different ways.

The *stolen* object is one that has found a home having gone through the phases of retrieval, conservation and collection, but has then been illegally removed from that home. Specialist collectors may place 'orders' for items already owned elsewhere, sometimes in museums or churches and often from other private collections. The *looted* object is one taken from its context of discovery, usually an archaeological site. Professional looters – such as the *tomboroli* (tomb robbers) of Italy (Thoden van Velzen, 1996) – are often excellent fieldworkers in their own right, seeking out sites of which the archaeological community is unaware. Other looters – sometimes professional, sometimes amateur – use metal detectors for treasure hunting on sites known to produce artefacts. Where there is poverty in an area, the discovery of a major archaeological site yielding interesting artefacts can lead to a new industry among the population: that of clandestine looting. Very often, such people claim a deep interest and indeed love of the past. The tomboroli, the treasure hunter and the local community often show a deep reverence for the sites they exploit and are keenly interested in the items they retrieve as historical objects. What they do not share is the archaeologist's claim to be the sole arbiter of the future of such objects and they see no objection to their sale for profit. The *illegally exported* object is one that may have been stolen or looted, but may also be legitimately owned. Many nations of the world, however, impose restrictions on the movements of certain types of object from one country to another. Where this is the case, it may be illegal to export an object on change of ownership, for the object to follow the owner around the globe or to arrange the sale of the object in one of the major markets in London or New York.

The existence of a market has in itself been held to be responsible for the destruction of valuable archaeological evidence. Renfrew (1993) accuses collectors of being 'the real looters'; and he accuses them of 'fraud' deriving from the loss to scholars and museums of the *'context of discovery'* of an object that appears in the salerooms (Renfrew, 1995: 8, emphasis in original). Others seek to ameliorate the effect of the trade in illicitly acquired antiquities by various means. One approach consists in carefully distinguishing the trade *per se* from a specifically *illicit* one by a strict reading of international laws (Cook, 1991: 536). Another recommends a market-price distinction between fully documented and unprovenanced items, with the latter priced at a significantly lower level (Cannon-Brookes, 1994: 350). A third urges the redirection of museum and collectors' funds towards 'long-term loans of objects, to the care and study of original material or the conservation of monuments *in situ*, to help with the protection of archaeologically and environmentally sensitive landscapes in economically disadvantaged countries, to the training of local academic and conservation experts' (Isler-Kerényi, 1994: 352). While, if workable, none of these initiatives should be dismissed – and Renfrew also recommends a strict application of legal regulation by museums and auction houses (Renfrew, 1995: 8–9) – the problem is less one of law than of differing ideologies.

Merryman (1989) has put an analysis of the types of value applicable to antiquities to effective use in his campaign for a 'licit' trade in cultural objects: he recognizes the change of context involved in bringing an ancient object into the present, since 'much of what we value today as cultural property originally had a religious function' (Merryman, 1989: 351). He lists the 'utility' of such objects as those of learning about the past, giving pleasure and enriching life, as a form of (economic/financial) wealth, and as tourist assets (also related to money) (Merryman, 1989: 353–5). He lists the components of effective cultural property policies to be: 'preservation', although he believes this is sometimes taken too far (Merryman, 1989: 355–8); 'truth' in the form of ensuring the authenticity of the object (Merryman, 1989: 359–60); ensuring 'access' to the object by scholars and others (Merryman, 1989: 360); and 'cultural nationalism' which 'has a disproportionate influence in cultural policy' (Merryman, 1989: 361–3). Against the current cultural property regime – which he argues to be 'nationalist [and] retensionist' (Merryman, 1994: 2) – he recommends the establishment of a specifically *licit* trade in antiquities, governed by international law (Merryman, 1994: 34–5). This trade would be in specifically 'movable' objects, defined as those which can be moved abroad without 'danger' to themselves; and in 'redundant' archaeological objects, which do not require to be held in a museum for the purposes of study (Merryman, 1994: 36). A trade in objects legitimately acquired but illegally exported would also be allowed, since illegal exportation is distinguishable from illegal acquisition and a matter for national law only (Merryman, 1994: 31). The structure of the trade would allow for both barter and a cash market (Merryman, 1994: 38–42) on the grounds that 'market price and value ... are not identical notions. ... But market price is an *indicator* of value, often the only or the best available indicator. ... [The licit international] market provides a medium for a substantial flow of efficient transactions' (Merryman, 1994: 41).

Merryman's argument is thus, at root, economic and legalistic: because a trade is physically possible and allowed by the rules, he suggests, it should come into being. He suggests that such a trade will have the desired effect of reducing 'clandestine archaeology' through effectively reducing the demand for illicitly produced items by feeding a legitimate market (Merryman, 1994: 42–52). He assumes throughout that any object brought to the market will find a buyer and, in taking an economic line of argument, he fails to consider the effect on demand of an increase in supply: these objects are not 'necessities' on which expenditure can be expected to remain constant (Douglas and Isherwood, 1979: 97–8) and so the market will respond differently. Finally, in attempting to resolve the problem of the illicit trade in antiquities and the 'retensionist' policies of states, Merryman does not challenge the basis on which these phenomena operate but instead responds in kind: to a problem of 'ownership' he responds with an increase of ownership opportunities.

Archaeological responses to the damage done by the looting of sites are to try to limit private collecting. The free-market lawyer's response is to increase ownership opportunities by restricting the notion of 'illicit'. Both responses treat archaeological remains as objects of value and, by so doing avoid the real argument. This is between different understandings of what the objects represent. For the archaeologist, they represent sources of information about the past; for the dealer they represent valuable commodities. These two different understandings are irreconcilable and represent completely different discourses, the one from scholarship, the other from economics. Any discussion between archaeologists and lawyers on this issue is likely to founder because each is talking about a fundamentally different understanding of what is at stake. When archaeologists try to argue on the grounds of the value of objects or on rights of ownership, they are also bound to fail: law and economics are the realms in which such ideas have meaning; archaeology is about things that are very different.

Buildings, sites and monuments

Buildings, sites and monuments are distinct heritage categories and yet have certain attributes in common, which make them convenient to discuss together. All are fixed in space – they cannot be lifted and carried around, which makes them different from portable objects - and they are neatly bounded. Buildings have external walls and usually a roof covering the interior. Sites extend only so far in space and it is possible to say '*here* is the site' and beyond that 'here is *not* the site'. Monuments are similarly bounded, either by physical external features, such as walls, ditches or banks, or by constructed fences or walls, or conceptually by agreement as to where the space of the monument comes to an end and the rest of the world takes over. Sometimes drawing the boundary is not particularly easy. Whereas a building has external walls, it may sit inside a garden or other space, and a decision will need to be taken whether or not to include this as part of the space occupied by the building. A site or a monument may have clear integral edges to it, such as an outer ditch, but material related to the site or activities within it may spill out beyond such features into the space beyond. This material may not cluster particularly clearly and may diminish gradually as it gets further from the site. In such a case, any boundary drawn will be an arbitrary choice rather than clearly dictated by the physical nature of the site itself.

A further attribute of buildings, sites and monuments is that they can – in some measure – be considered interchangeable. A building can be classed as a monument or a site and, if ruined, will generally be classified as the latter. The site of a (former) building can be classed either as a site or as a monument or even as both. The position of a monument can be classified as its site, and a site in archaeological usage (to be discussed below) may be located on a monument. Despite their shared attributes and interchangeability, however, the three categories are not quite identical. In particular, the origin of the term for each is different, the function they serve is different and, as heritage, their fate may vary.

[handwritten margin note: not always true / bldgs can be moved]

BUILDINGS

The term 'building' as used in heritage is usually a shorthand word for 'standing building in use'. This excludes structures without walls or roofs, ruined or abandoned structures or the sites of now-vanished structures. The latter will be classed as monuments or sites. Buildings are thus structures with external walls and a roof containing space to be used for one or several of a variety of possible purposes – whether domestic, industrial, administrative, ritual, political or religious. In general, to be classed as 'heritage' a building will either need to be considered historic (that is, beyond a certain age) or historical (associated with a particular historic event or person), although these can conflate where the historical relates to a reasonably distant past. The 'historic building' is accordingly a particular class of heritage object and subject to a particular type of treatment.

The prerequisite of a historic building is that it must be preserved. Efforts will therefore be set in train to ensure that its physical fabric does not deteriorate. The first stage of this is usually to place it on a list of such protected objects which will – at least notionally – prevent harmful actions from being taken against it. It may be subject also to a degree of rehabilitation or reconstruction – usually to return it to a physical condition deemed appropriate. This very often means 'fixing' it in the condition it was in at a particular moment in its history, by removing later additions and accretions and restoring lost features. Such protection and alteration often only applies to the exterior of a building: since it will remain in use, the interior must be suitable for modern purposes and so heating, ventilation and internal arrangements must meet modern expectations and the health and safety requirements currently in force. Internal features which match the historic nature of the building and indeed contribute to its 'authenticity' – a quality as ascribed in relation to a building as to any other object - may be lost in such a process unless specifically accorded protection. The end result is an ancient structure suitable for modern use, ensuring the survival into the future of at least the external fabric.

Such modern use is unlikely to match the original use: former churches can become community halls or private homes; former workshops, warehouses and factories can become homes; former homes can become museums or shops. The process of transformation is usually called 'adaptive re-use' and is considered entirely appropriate for old buildings considered worth keeping.

MONUMENTS

Strictly speaking, the category 'monument' is not an archaeological but a legal one: it is therefore more 'heritage' than archaeology. Historically, the term was used not to denote standing features of earth or stone, but written documents from past ages. In the nineteenth century the term began to include all or any ancient made thing – whether portable or fixed – including documents and written texts. Only towards the end of that century did the idea of monument as a large fixed structure gain prominence and application of the term to written materials cease to apply. In Britain at least, adoption of the term from 1880 onwards as the legal description for large built landscape features worthy of some form of protection fixed the meaning we know today. In general, monuments as understood today are held to be fixed landscape features, where the emphasis is placed upon the external surface. Whereas buildings have interiors and exteriors and the focus is upon their function and sites have depth in the form of stratigraphy, monuments have solidity and shape.

The term 'monument' is perhaps the broadest category applied to heritage objects. It can include not only ruins and buried features but also be applied to standing buildings and indeed what are otherwise called sites. In the guise of 'national monument' (a designation used widely across the world) it can cover anything from a single-standing feature to an entire landscape: accordingly, even the miles-wide battlefields of North America and Europe fall under this category. There are, however, limitations placed upon what can today constitute a monument. It generally has to be something which stands on, penetrates or is made out of the ground where it is located. It has to be clearly distinguishable from that ground, in the form of upstanding features or depressions. Much archaeological material does not take this form and so cannot be a monument in this sense: flint or other material scatters, for example, cannot be easily distinguished from the soil of which they are a part, nor do they stand upon or penetrate that soil. Nevertheless, such features are archaeological and often provide significant evidence for past human activity in an area.

Like a building, a monument is usually accorded a measure of protection and, also like a building, will be placed on a list of similar such structures. This will prevent removal, damage or other interference. Occasionally some measure of reconstruction may be undertaken, to restore the monument to a condition held to have applied at some point in its past, often to give visitors and viewers some idea of its original appearance. This is not, however, adaptive re-use because the purpose of a monument is generally to be simply a monument from – or to – the past, rather than to have a modern function.

SITES

The concept of the 'site' in archaeology is not a particularly simple one and is rarely discussed (cf. Dunnell, 1992). The focus of attention is more often placed upon its internal structure, in the form of stratigraphy representing activities at the site separated by time, as revealed in the process of archaeological work (Harris, 1979; Hodder, 1999; Lucas, 2001).

The concept 'site' as used in archaeology has two meanings, rarely separated in archaeological discourse and often conflated. The first relates to material as found in the present: this is the site as the object of attention of archaeologists today. The second relates to the past: this is the site as the location of human activity in that past. It is likely that the site of human activity in the past – an ancient field system, a settlement site, a ritual monument or a defensive structure – may become the focus of archaeological investigation in the present. It is also possible, however, that taphonomic phenomena may remove material from one location to another: material deposited in a stream, for example, may be moved downstream by water action and deposited on the stream bank; or material deposited on an ancient beach may be included in an eroding cliff face and fall out onto the modern beach surface. In the latter cases, although the focus of archaeological attention, the site is not that of the human activity represented by the material.

Sites are usually not sites in and of themselves but the site *of* something else: of some kind of activity, such as archaeology; of a former object or structure, such as a now-ruined building; or of something still extant, such as a monument. Sites do not, therefore, stand alone and cannot be understood or comprehended without taking into account this additional qualifying attribute. This distinguishes them from buildings and monuments, since these terms represent objects that need no qualifier. A monument can be clearly understood as a monument without requiring a designation as a particular kind of monument; and a building can be comprehended as a building regardless of the function for which it was built or is currently used. A site, however, is usually considered to be the *site of* something.

Sites are capable of protection from alteration, damage or change of use. Often this involves their designation as something else: usually a monument or a building. Sites can also, however, be subject to other treatments. Investigation of a site often involves its excavation, either in whole or part. Such investigation inevitably involves the destruction of the site and its reduction to a set of records in the form of an excavation report. This will in turn be supported by the site archive: the records made on site and materials (small finds and samples) recovered. Alternatively, if not considered worthy of investigation, a site may be abandoned to its fate: often this too will involve eventual destruction, through construction work or other damaging activity.

PROTECTIVE CATEGORIES

Table 1.6 set out the key practices of heritage management – the things that those responsible for the material heritage actually do. The processes of identification and inventory depend upon the availability of categories into which to place material. The process of evaluation – whereby the suitability of an object for a particular fate is established – leads to the final decision as to its future. Where the outcome for a site is its preservation, this is often by way of suitably designating the site as something other than a site: in the UK, sites thus become 'monuments'; elsewhere, they may become 'National Monuments'; for the grandest sites, designation as a 'World Heritage Site' is a possibility. Alternative outcomes include abandonment - in which case the fate of the object is left very much to chance or the perfidy of others; and 'rescue' by excavation, sometimes known as 'preservation by record'.

There are various kinds of possible categories in which buildings and monuments may be placed for protection from harm, both in the UK and wider afield. *Buildings* in the UK may be 'listed' – that is, placed upon a list of nationally prized buildings – which protects them from certain kinds of change. Often this is limited to the exterior of the building, although it can include certain interior features. There is no change in ownership involved but certain changes of use may be specifically excluded. Listed buildings qualify for state grants for upkeep and maintenance. *Monuments* in the UK are subject to two main types of legally sanctioned protection. As 'scheduled monuments' deemed to be of 'national importance' they are given (at least in theory) protection from all harm. No change of ownership of the monument or the land on which it stands is involved, and no right of public access is included, but neither the owner nor anyone else is entitled to alter or damage the monument without the prior written consent of the relevant Government minister. Alternatively, a 'monument in guardianship' is physically protected from harm for the purpose of public access. As with scheduling, no change in ownership takes place but the State or a local authority takes upon itself all responsibility for the monument and its maintenance, care and protection, and the owner too may qualify for grants for upkeep and maintenance. Internationally sites, monuments, buildings and landscapes can be classed as *'National Monuments'*. This marks them as sites of high status, offers a high degree of protection for the purpose of public access and, in addition, they usually qualify for State funding for maintenance, upkeep and management. *World Heritage* status derives from international agreements (see Chapter 3) giving international recognition to the site which must meet stringent international standards. Although in terms of protection usually no more is offered than is provided already by national law, international sources of funding become available for upkeep and management of the site.

All such designations share certain things in common. All aim to protect the object from alteration or change: in effect, they 'freeze' it at a particular moment in its history. In more extreme applications – where a measure of 'restoration' is undertaken – the object is not only frozen at a particular moment but reconstructed to conform with an expectation of what it 'should' look like. The designations also give the site a certain status: indeed, this is one of the purposes underlying the protection of old things: it is to mark them as important or significant (see Chapter 6 for more on this).

PROBLEMS WITH 'MONUMENTS'

General adoption in Britain of the term 'monument' for those archaeological objects to be protected has led to the charge of 'monumental thinking' being levelled at heritage managers (Carver, 1996). Monuments are, it is argued, a different kind of thing from an archaeological site. The latter is a locus of research into the past and that is its value: its function is therefore to be researched, which may mean excavating it out of existence. The benefit of doing so is that knowledge of the past is enriched and enlarged. By contrast, monuments are objects that sit in the landscape surrounding them. Their function is to be preserved as landscape features. They, therefore, may provide a source of amenity and aesthetic value but tell us nothing about the past, which is the purpose of archaeology. Accordingly, to treat objects of archaeological attention as monuments is to deny their archaeological status. In effect, treating sites as monuments removes them from the archaeological realm altogether and places them on a par with other kinds of static heritage object. As such, they are no longer able to fulfil the function required of an archaeological site, which is to be investigated. Monuments are therefore more similar to an unused but viable building than an archaeological site: another way in which these categories are – to some extent – interchangeable.

The problems of 'monumental thinking' are particularly evident in dealing with sites that are non-monumental in nature. Monumental structures appear relatively late in human history and much of the human past - from the emergence of the earliest hominids to the epipalaeolithic or mesolithic periods – is represented by more ephemeral bodies of material. Typically, they compose flint or bone scatters, areas interpreted as 'hunting and gathering ranges' or the sites of temporary or more permanent 'camps' rather than 'settlements' (cf. Carman, 1999c: 24). Rarely can they be considered as fixed and bounded points in a landscape and certainly not 'monumental' unless they are painted caves or rock-shelters: not infrequently, such sites as these are treated as 'art' rather than 'archaeology' by the application of formal methods of analysis (Chippindale and Taçon 1998). In addition, since the more ephemeral most ancient sites have not been 'built' in the conventional sense, they do not constitute monuments and tend therefore to fall outside conventional approaches to conservation and protection (Wenban-Smith, 1995). Moreover, for heritage purposes, they are frequently considered more 'natural' than 'cultural' in form and thus not strictly 'archaeological' at all. All of this tends to leave them outside the concerns of conventional heritage management practice which are the product of the 'monumental thinking' criticized by Carver (1996).

Landscapes

As well as being considered a 'container' for other things (Tables 2.1 and 2.2), a landscape in both archaeological and heritage thinking is often also considered to be more about 'nature' than about 'culture'. Unlike portable objects, landscapes are not considered to be made; unlike buildings, sites and monuments, they are not considered to be constructed or built. Accordingly, landscapes represent the 'natural backdrop' against which culture takes place, an idea congruent with early processual archaeologies concerned with economic and ecological models for interpreting the human past, which treated the environment solely as a resource to be exploited (Higgs, 1972; Higgs, 1975; Jarman *et al.*, 1982; Butzer, 1982). An alternative vision of landscapes as at least partly human-made, however, may be more realistic and helpful (Darvill, 1987). In such an approach, there is no such thing as a 'natural' landscape: in interpreting landscape, the focus is placed upon the role of human activity in shaping it.

Moreover, as a number of commentators have pointed out and as Thomas (1993, 21–6) and Darvill (1996) have discussed from an archaeological perspective, any landscape is also essentially the

Table 2.5 Landscape types

Semi-natural landscapes	Wetlands
	Estuaries
	Rivers/lakes/alluvial spreads
Human-made landscapes	Grassland
	Woodland
	Lowland heath
	Upland moor
	Arable land
	Parkland/ornamental garden

Source: Darvill, 1987

focus and creation of the modern *gaze*: 'In contemporary Western societies [landscape is] only the surface of the land. ... It is ... an ego-centred landscape, perspectival landscape, a landscape of views as vistas' (Bender, 1993: 1). In other words, there is a very real sense in which an objective landscape, divorced from the process of interpreting space, can never exist. Any landscape is, instead, only what a particular individual can see from a particular point in space and, if that individual moves position, a different landscape is thereby created. 'Heritage' landscapes are, therefore, also created – and to some extent also inevitably invented – spaces. This is particularly true of the landscape in its domesticated guise as 'countryside' (Fowler, 1995; Williamson and Bellamy, 1987) and as a space the meaning of which 'is grounded in existential or lived consciousness of it' (Tilley, 1994: 15).

TYPES OF HERITAGE LANDSCAPE

Heritage landscapes across the world generally fall into two types. There are those landscapes which fall very firmly into Darvill's category of 'built' landscapes: these include urban space; parkland and gardens, where nature is directly transformed (and indeed re-formed) by the human hand; and the sites of particular historical events, such as 'historic battlefields'. There are also those which – although in practice the result of human activity over time – are considered 'natural': among these are those sometimes very extensive areas of land designated as 'National Parks', 'Wilderness Areas', 'Heritage Coasts' or 'National Forests'. A newer idea is that of the 'archaeological park' which recognizes the cultural nature of ancient remains but seeks to make them accessible in the same way as nature.

Towns are readily recognized as cultural spaces created by human activity with very little of the 'natural' about them. Inside such urban areas certain spaces are capable of recognition as particularly 'cultural' and worthy of note and therefore of a measure of preservation. The focus in such spaces is primarily upon externals: the fabric of buildings, the look of the space, its atmosphere and 'character'. In preserving such things, the focus is often upon the aesthetic qualities of a space rather than its uses in history. Previously industrial spaces can be converted into areas for habitation and previously inhabited spaces into commercial areas. This is very close to the manner in which individual buildings are usually treated as parts of the heritage: although taking cognisance of the way in which buildings interrelate, the space as a whole is treated rather as one would treat a single structure, focusing upon adaptive reuse and external appearance.

Gardens, battlefields and similar kinds of space are usually the product of activity among the rich and powerful in the past: they represent 'high' history and elite status. They correspond closely with 'monumental' notions of heritage, which tend to concentrate on large structures such as prehistoric ritual sites built of earth and/ or stone, ancient and now ruined cities, defensive works, large religious centres and aristocratic country houses. They share with monuments and sites the ability to have a convenient boundary placed around them so that they may be marked off from the rest of the world. In the case of a garden or park, the boundary will be a physical one such as a wall or a ditch: inside is the park or garden, outside is not. A battlefield does not come so readily distinguished from its surrounding context, but it is possible to identify those spaces where battlefield action took place and so to draw a continuous line around such spaces: inside the line is considered to be the area of battle, outside is not. This ability to mark and separate the space from other contiguous space lends itself to the process of inventory and commonly such heritage spaces will be placed on a list or register which also marks them as 'heritage' spaces. Once so marked and bounded, consideration can be given to restoring them to a past condition and to their use, especially for the provision of public access (Pearson and Sullivan, 1995: 236–8).

Spaces marked out on the basis that they represent the best 'nature' has to offer are also frequently treated as such to make them available for the wider public. These do not represent an 'elite' history, however, but were often created as spaces for clean and healthy recreation for the benefit of an otherwise urban industrial population. Their promotion as entirely natural places is an integral part of their creation and purpose and so any archaeology they contain is very often treated as an 'accidental extra' rather than as an integral part of their form. Accordingly the inhabitants of such areas are usually deemed to live a rural existence or one 'in tune with nature' – despite the presence of and their direct involvement in activities such as mining, quarrying or other industrial activity. In accordance with this general principle, in the USA, where large tracts of land were set aside as National Parks from the mid-nineteenth century onwards, the indigenous population were allowed continued residence. As a result, they too were relegated to being treated as part of 'nature' rather than allowed a fully-fledged cultural existence, a condition reflected by the treatment of their physical remains (Hubert, 1989; to be discussed further in Chapter 5). Similarly, in Australia, members of the indigenous population are only given recognition as truly indigenous if they inhabit areas away from towns and do not engage in industries or activities considered the province of the European majority (Smith, 2000; Lee Long, 2000).

Recent note has been taken of the close affinity between the way in which certain cultural materials and some elements of the natural world are treated (Holtorf, 2001). Specifically, this gives rise to the suggestion that 'public' archaeology (see Chapters 4 and 5) should adopt some of the methods and approaches to presentation adopted in zoos and similar institutions. Other affinities exist between the treatments of culture and nature, however, and especially in the manner in which certain large-scale archaeological sites are treated. These 'archaeological parks' – frequently urban sites, either in the past or both in past and present – are presented as spaces in which to wander in a manner similar to 'natural' places such as National

Parks and Wilderness Areas. Instead of enjoying majestic mountain or forested scenery, the visitor is encouraged to wonder at the constructive abilities of past cultures, treating the space as an 'open' environment rather than an enclosed site. Here notions of 'nature' and 'culture' – and of how we should react to them – are merged.

Conceptions of the heritage

Portable objects are solid and the form does not change. Sites, buildings and monuments are fixed in space and have boundaries – physical or conceptual – placed around them. Similarly, landscape spaces such as urban conservation areas, historic gardens and historic battlefields are enclosed spaces in which the cultural aspects of the place are emphasized over and above any natural features or qualities it possesses. By contrast, in more open spaces, archaeology and culture are subsumed within nature. In the former, nature is transformed into culture in the same way that an object is made or a building, monument or site constructed; in the latter, culture is treated as part of nature. This tells us something about how we comprehend the human past and is a central part of heritage practices. Whereas 'nature' – also sometimes called 'the environment' – is ubiquitous and all-encompassing, 'culture' is deemed to be enclosed and bounded. Where heritage is treated as all-encompassing nature, however, it is often not entirely treated as cultural: accordingly, indigenous populations are relegated to aspects of the natural environment and find themselves objects of study and the place where they are studied to be the museum of nature rather than of culture.

Further reading

Portable objects

Clifford, J. (1988) *The Predicament of Culture: Twentieth-century Ethnography, Literature and Art.* Cambridge, MA: Harvard University Press.
Pearce, S. M. (1992) *Museums, Objects and Collections: A Cultural Study.* Leicester: Leicester University Press.

Pearce, S. M. (1995) *On Collecting: An Investigation into Collecting in the European Tradition*. Collecting Cultures. London: Routledge.

Renfrew, C. (1993) 'Collectors are the real looters', *Archaeology* (May/June 1993), 16.

Renfrew, C. (2001) *Loot, Legitimacy and Ownership*. Duckworth Debates in Archaeology. London: Duckworth.

Buildings, monuments and sites

Carver, M. (1996) 'On archaeological value', *Antiquity* 70: 45–56.

Freeman, P. and Pollard, T. (eds) (2001) *Fields of Conflict: Progress and Prospects in Battlefield Archaeology*. Oxford: BAR.

Harris, E. C. (1979) *Principles of Archaeological Stratigraphy*. London: Academic Press.

Hodder, I. (1999)*The Archaeological Process*. Oxford: Blackwell.

Lucas, G. (2001) *Critical Approaches to Fieldwork: Contemporary and Historical Archaeological Practice*. London: Routledge.

Wenban-Smith, F. (1995) 'Square pegs in round holes: problems of managing the Palaeolithic heritage', in M. Cooper, A. Firth, J. Carman and D. Wheatley (eds) *Managing Archaeology*. TAG. London: Routledge, 146–62.

Landscapes

Brown, A. E. (1991) *Garden Archaeology*. CBA Research Report 78. London: CBA.

Countryside Commission (1989) *A People's Charter: Forty Years of the National Parks and Access to the Countryside Act 1949*. London: HMSO.

Darvill, T. (1987) *Ancient Monuments in the Countryside: An Archaeological Management Review*. English Heritage Archaeological Report 5. London: English Heritage.

Darvill, T., Gerrard, G. and Startin, B. (1993) 'Identifying and protecting historic landscapes', *Antiquity* 67: 563–74.

Jones, M. and Rotherham, D. (eds) (1998) *Landscapes – Perception, Recognition and Management: Reconciling the Impossible? Landscape Archaeology and Ecology* 2. Sheffield: Landscape Conservation Forum.

Summary points

1. The heritage is constructed out of various kinds of objects which are deemed appropriate for heritage status. In general, these in turn fall into the three major categories of: portable object; building, site or monument; and landscape.
2. The three main heritage categories are usually considered to form a hierarchy, moving from smaller to larger, or – down the scale of size – from container to contained. They are also, in general, subject to different styles of treatment.
3. Portable objects are removed from their contexts and become parts of owned collections. In museums, they acquire the quality of 'authenticity'. As part of a private collection they may be subject to theft or trading in the market for antiquities. As elements in a collection, their function is to support an idea about identity, whether collective (in the museum) or individual (in private hands).
4. Buildings, sites and monuments are distinguishable from their surroundings and have boundaries placed around them. They are subject to preservation without change in ownership status. Where 'monumental thinking' predominates, otherwise archae-ologically important (but not particularly monumental) sites may find themselves outside the preservation and management process.
5. Although considered 'natural', landscapes are always largely created by human action: indeed, any identified landscape is the product of a particular point of view. Various kinds of landscape can be included as 'heritage places', ranged along a scale from those considered most 'cultural' (such as gardens and battle-fields) to those considered more 'natural' (such as wilderness spaces).

The built heritage

Plate 2.1 The great octagonal keep at Orford Castle, Suffolk, England

Plate 2.2 Medieval gatehouse and merchant's house, Southampton, England

Plate 2.3 Agia Sofia, Istanbul, Turkey (fifth-century Christian church, sixteenth-century mosque and modern museum)

Plate 2.4 Colonial-style church, Venezuela

Plate 2.5 'Cape Dutch' architecture, Stellenbosch, South Africa

3 Institutions of Heritage

Heritage objects – whether portable objects, monuments and sites, or landscapes – are the responsibility of particular kinds of organizations. Some of these exist at the international and, indeed, global level, some at the level of individual nation states, while others are regional or local. Many are bureaucracies of one kind or another – an idea to be addressed in Chapter 4 – concerned with administration and the application of regimes of legal regulation, while the museum is a particular kind of institution universally recognized. Not all organizations concerned with heritage are exclusively concerned with cultural matters and some – while exclusively cultural in terms of concern – have remits that extend well beyond the heritage alone. This chapter will outline the work of various kinds of heritage organization, especially those which have an 'official' or legally sanctioned existence.

There are inevitable differences between these organizations in terms of specific internal structure, governing authority, areas of responsibility, powers and duties. This reflects both the different levels at which they operate – global, regional, national, local – and differences of culture between one part of the world and another. At the same time, however, there is an underlying similarity between them all in terms of purpose and function. This in turn reflects the nature of heritage practice as something common to the world as a whole. Those officially responsible for the heritage share, for good or ill, a common appreciation of what a heritage is supposed to be, what it is for and how it should be treated. This in turn contributes towards the paradox of heritage mentioned in Chapter 1: that heritage is a field of complexity that results in a few simple practices.

Heritage organizations

Neither the UN (the United Nations) nor its daughter organization UNESCO (the United Nations Educational, Scientific and Cultural Organization) is exclusively – nor indeed primarily - an organization devoted to heritage concerns. The primary duty of both is to promote international stability and cooperation: UNESCO as a member organization of the UN is concerned with achieving this in the realms of education, science and culture. Both are organizations of which individual nation states are the members, together with a number of international 'non-governmental organizations' (NGOs) staffed by professionals in various fields. Among those NGOs recognized by UNESCO are:

> The International Council of Museums (ICOM)
> The International Committee for Monuments and Sites (ICOMOS)
> The ICOMOS International Committee on Archaeological Heritage Management (ICAHM).

Tables 3.1 and 3.2 set out the 'familial' relationships between these organizations and their purposes and functions as they describe them. Not surprisingly, perhaps, the more general objectives – peace and security, common welfare, the establishment of human rights – are the province of the UN and UNESCO: the more specialist heritage functions are those of the bodies further down the hierarchy. It is, however, notably *as* a hierarchy that these organizations are arranged and this pattern is also reflected at the regional and national levels.

Table 3.1 Relations between global heritage bodies

Parent	Child	Related NGO	Specialist committee
United Nations	UNESCO	ICOM	
		ICOMOS	ICAHM

Table 3.2 Functions of global bodies

Organization*	Purpose/functions
United Nations (www.un.org)	To *maintain international peace and security* through collective measures to prevent or remove threats to the peace and to suppress aggression and other breaches of the peace *Peaceful settlement* of international disputes, in conformity with the principles of justice and international law To *develop friendly relations* among nations, based upon respect for the principle of equal rights and self-determination of peoples, and to take measures to strengthen universal peace To *achieve international co-operation* in solving international economic, social, cultural or humanitarian problems To *promote and encourage respect for human rights* and fundamental freedoms for all without distinction as to race, sex, language or religion
UNESCO (United Nations Educational, Scientific and Cultural Organization) (www.unesco.org)	To contribute to *peace and security* in the world by promoting *collaboration* among nations through education, science, culture and communication in order to further universal respect for justice, for the rule of law and for the human rights and fundamental freedoms which are affirmed for the peoples of the world, without distinction of race, sex, language or religion, by the Charter of the United Nations *Functions:* *Prospective studies*: what forms of education, science, culture and communication for tomorrow's world? *The advancement, transfer and sharing of knowledge*: relying primarily on research, training and teaching activities *Standard-setting* action: the preparation and adoption of international instruments and statutory recommendations

Table 3.2 – *continued*

Organization*	Purpose/functions
	Expertise: provided to member states for their development policies and projects in the form of 'technical co-operation' Exchange of specialized information
ICOMOS (International Committee on Monuments and Sites) (www. international. icomos.org)	To bring together conservation specialists from all over the world and serve as a forum for professional *dialogue and exchange* To *collect, evaluate and disseminate information* on conservation principles, techniques and policies To *co-operate* with national and international authorities on the establishment of documentation centres specializing in conservation To *work for the adoption and implementation of international conventions* on the conservation and enhancement of architectural heritage To participate in the organization of *training programmes* for conservation specialists on a worldwide scale To put *expertise* of highly qualified professionals and specialists at the service of the international community
ICOM (International Council of Museums) (www.icom.org)	The *promotion and development of museums* and the museum profession at an international level
ICAHM (ICOMOS International Committee on Archaeological Heritage Management) (B. Egloff and	The fundamental purpose of *stimulating the widest understanding of the importance of the archaeological* heritage among the general public and government institutions The promotion of the *systematic inventory* of the world's archaeological heritage The development of efficient and sympathetic *strategies for the management* of that heritage for the

Table 3.2 – *continued*

Organization*	Purpose/functions
T. Wheaton, pers. comm.)	long-term benefit of both scientists and the general public
	The encouragement of *a multidisciplinary approach* to the cultural heritage
	The *improvement of methods and standards* among those concerned with archaeological heritage management, i.e. by striving towards compatibility of documentation, establishing minimum standards for sampling procedures, recording and publication, etc.
	The establishing of *minimum standards* for the training and qualification of those engaged in archaeological heritage management
	The encouragement of the *exchange of experience and expertise* in the field of archaeological heritage management.

* The source of information about each organization is given in parentheses.

Accordingly, out of a basic concern for international security and the application of common rights to all humanity comes a concern for the care and regulation of the human past. At this level, the focus is placed very strongly – and indeed legitimately – upon international co-operation in this field. Much is made of the establishment and exchange of expertise and knowledge and setting minimum standards of performance. So much of this expertise and knowledge derives from Western traditions of professionalism and also largely rests upon Western notions of what constitutes a heritage in the first place. Accordingly, this provides the basis for the charge of the West attempting to levy a 'global imperialism' on the rest of the world by way of archaeological heritage practices (Byrne, 1991).

Not only global organizations are concerned with heritage issues, however, since this interest in the cultural is echoed at the regional and national levels of organization. The Organization of American

States (OAS) seeks to achieve for the Americas what the UN aims to do for the world. In Europe, responsibility for heritage at the continental level is split between two bodies. The Council of Europe is primarily concerned with issues of culture while the European Union is primarily concerned with economic and political issues (Tables 3.3 and 3.4). Inevitably, however, the EU finds itself involved in cultural matters by attempting to create a common European sense of identity built around its member states; this is achieved by the creation of a limited amount of legislation but primarily by other policy decisions and declarations (Tzanidaki, 2000).

Table 3.3 Areas covered by regional heritage bodies

Europe		*Americas*
Council of Europe	European Union	Organization of American States

Table 3.4 Functions of regional bodies

Body	*Functions*
Council of Europe (www.coe.org)	To *protect human rights, pluralist democracy and the rule of law; to promote awareness and encourage the development of Europe's cultural identity* and diversity To *seek solutions to problems* facing European society (discrimination against minorities, xenophobia, intolerance, environmental protection, human cloning, AIDS, drugs, organized crime, etc.) To *help consolidate democratic stability* in Europe by backing political, legislative and constitutional reform
European Union (www.fco.gov.org)	To *protect the rights and interests of its citizens*: maintain freedom, security and justice; promote prosperity, jobs and development; and act effectively on the international scene

Table 3.4 – *continued*

Body	Functions
	To *establish a single market*: ensuring free movement of goods, peoples, services and field for business
	To *establish common policies* on agriculture, fisheries, transport, environment, etc.
	To *establish co-operation* and/or coordination in economic policies, industry, employment, consumer protection, etc.
	To *work together* to fight cross-border crime, drugs and terrorism and to control external borders, asylum and immigration
	To *act together* in foreign policy, to preserve peace and promote international co-operation
Organization of American States (www.oas.org)	To *strengthen the peace* and security of the continent
	To *promote and consolidate representative democracy*, with due respect for the principle of non-intervention
	To *prevent possible causes of difficulties* and to ensure the pacific settlement of disputes that may arise among the member states
	To *provide for common action* on the part of those states in the event of aggression
	To *seek the solution of political, juridical and economic problems* that may arise among them
	To *promote, by cooperative action*, their economic, social, and cultural development
	To *eradicate extreme poverty*, which constitutes an obstacle to the full democratic development of the peoples of the hemisphere
	To *achieve an effective limitation of conventional weapons* that will make it possible to devote the largest amount of resources to the economic and social development of the member states

Organizations and laws

The UN, UNESCO, the Council of Europe and the OAS operate by providing a forum in which issues of common concern can be debated and from which international legislation can then emerge. The latter (see Table 3.5) most often takes the form of a series of multilateral treaties requiring formal consent and ratification by individual nation states before they are binding on that government and its successors. Although binding upon governments, none of them is binding upon an individual or group within the jurisdiction of that government until it is incorporated into national law. The latter is very rare: in most cases, the international treaty is taken as a minimum standard against which national laws on heritage protection and management, and their administration, is measured. Conventions, Protocols and Charters are all such multilateral treaties binding upon governments; in contrast, Recommendations are adopted merely by a simple majority of member states voting in General Assembly and are taken to constitute a minimum standard of accepted practice.

The administration of such legislation at the global level is usually delegated to an appropriate NGO. Accordingly, responsibility for the day-to-day operation of the UNESCO Conventions on the protection of heritage in armed conflict, on the illicit movement of cultural property and on the World Heritage is delegated to ICOMOS and the UNESCO Recommendation on archaeological excavation is currently in the process of redrafting by ICAHM. Regional legislation usually remains the responsibility of the body creating it through its various committees and other organs and of individual nation states who are party to it. In Europe and the Americas a concern for the archaeological and cultural heritage is affirmed in Conventions, as they are at the global level. In Europe, Conventions tend to be the province of the Council of Europe which has a much looser structure than the EU. The latter can enforce its decisions on member states far more rigorously and so the legislation takes a different form: Directives are instruments requiring member states to legislate in a particular manner on a particular matter, while Regulations have immediate effect upon member states. While the European Commission – effectively the 'civil service' of the EU – oversees the general application of these laws and ensures compliance by member states, the application of the laws to particular cases is the responsibility of the member states themselves. This reflects in some manner the situation at the global level. Although Conventions, Charters and Recommendations represent the overarching global regulation of heritage matters, the international agencies alone have very few powers for their enforcement. Instead they rely upon member states to monitor their own and others' actions and to provide the necessary structures and resources to see that they are put into effect.

Table 3.5 International legislation on heritage and archaeology

Coverage	Date	Title
Global	1954	UNESCO Convention for the Protection of Cultural Property in the Event of Armed Conflict (Hague Convention)
	1956	UNESCO Recommendation on international principles applicable to archaeological excavations
	1966	International Charter for the Conservation and Restoration of Monuments and Sites
	1970	UNESCO Convention on the means of prohibiting and preventing the illicit import, export and transfer of ownership of cultural property (Paris Convention)
	1972	UNESCO Convention for the Protection of the World Cultural and Natural Heritage (World Heritage Convention)
	1972	UNESCO Recommendation concerning the protection, at a national level, of the cultural and natural heritage
Regional – Europe	1954	European Cultural Convention (CoE)
	1969/ 1992	European Convention on the Protection of the Archaeological Heritage (CoE)
	1992	Regulation on the export of cultural goods (EU)
	1992	Directive on the Return of Cultural Objects Unlawfully Removed from the Territory of a Member State (EU)
Regional – Americas	1976	OAS Convention on Protection of the Archaeological, Historical and Artistic Heritage of the American Nations

One of the problems commonly encountered with international laws is that they do not apply universally since they are only enforceable in favour of or against states which have chosen to join. Regional legislation, therefore, only covers the particular region where it operates. Globally, while most countries have signed up to the Convention for the protection of cultural property during wartime (the Hague Convention) and the World Heritage Convention, a significant number of others have not yet adopted the Convention relating to the illicit movement of cultural property (the Paris Convention). The Hague Convention is seen as a useful protection for one's own cultural heritage during times of conflict: it also stands as a measure of one's civilized and modern status and there are, therefore, considerable advantages in any State subscribing to it. The World Heritage Convention – which requires states to put forward possible candidates for the list of World Heritage sites – offers the chance to indicate the contribution of a country to global culture, putting it on a par with any other nation of the world. The Paris Convention provides for the return by one state to another of items illegally transported across its borders, but can only be enforced against states which have signed up to it. Prominent among those countries which have not yet signed the Paris Convention is the United Kingdom. The argument usually put forward for this is that the trade in antiquities based in London may be harmed; at the time of writing, however, the announcement has been made that the UK will be signing up in the near future.

Within Europe other problems are also emerging. The European Union is not primarily a cultural organization and so its legislative action in respect of cultural property relates to those items primarily as economic goods. In creating a single market in Europe, the EU must provide for the free movement of all goods within its borders. The transfer of heritage objects is not an issue on which it is qualified to legislate except in terms of freeing the movement of such items. Accordingly, its regulations on controlling the export of cultural property only concern their transfer across the European boundary to a country which is not a member of the EU: transfers between countries within the EU are not only allowed but – in economic terms at least - encouraged. Where a transfer is made illegally the Regulation on the return of cultural objects applies.

Where an object is in the course of transfer outside the EU, the Directive on the export of cultural property (and any national legislation of the exporting country deriving from it) applies. Since, however, it is the individual member state which has the responsibility for taking action, the possibility arises of the export from the EU of a heritage object valued as such by its country of origin but not by the country in which it presently resides. Only if the item has been transferred illegally from its country of origin will there be any provision for its retention in the EU.

In general, and despite (especially international and indeed much archaeological) rhetoric to the contrary, the arbiter of heritage practice across the world is the nation state. In the global arena, it is the state which provides international agencies with their powers and acts as their agent. At the level of the individual nation state, power is retained and exercised at the national level, although specific functions may be delegated to local bodies. The precise organization varies from state to state depending upon its own internal structure (Tables 3.6 and 3.7).

Federal states – such as the USA, Canada, Australia or Germany – may operate at two distinct levels: the overarching federal level, where interest (as to some extent in the USA, and in Canada, for instance) may be limited to areas where federal authority holds sway but not beyond; and at the level of the state or province where more generally applicable laws may be generated. In Germany, however – where individual states are also deemed to represent distinct cultures – there is no federal action regarding the heritage, and heritage laws operate only at the level of each state (Reichstein, 1984). Even where much authority to govern the heritage resides below the federal level – as in the USA, Canada or Australia – it can be central federal authority which determines the shape of heritage organization. In the USA, for instance, it is federal law which provides the framework within which the Historic Preservation Officer for each state (SHPO) operates. In Australia, the over-arching federal legislation provides the model most often applied in each state and federal heritage organization may be mirrored at the state level (Pearson and Sullivan, 1995: 44–76). In Canada, while the local level of heritage administration responds to the state minister responsible, federal authority generally restricts its

Table 3.6 Archaeological organization in the nation state: federal states

State	Federal level	State/province	Local
USA	National Park Service; Environmental Protection Agency	State Historic Preservation Officer	
Canada	Parks Canada Archaeological Survey of Canada	State Minister	Municipal officer Regional archaeologist
Germany		State Monument Service	
Australia	Australian Heritage Commission	Heritage Council Historic Buildings Council	

Table 3.7 Archaeological organization in the nation state: unitary states

State	National level	County/département/ region/province/ prefecture	Local
UK	English Heritage (England) Cadw (Wales) Historic Scotland (Scotland)	County Archaeological Officer	Local volunteer society Museum
France	Antiquities service	Local authority Museum	
Denmark	Ancient Monuments Administration National Museum	Regional museum University	
Japan	Centre for Archaeological Operations	Prefectural board for education Regional museum	University Museum
India	Archaeological Survey of India	Superintendant of Archaeology	Archaeologist

concern to places of significance to Canada as a whole. In unitary (non-federal) states the overarching authority usually resides at the national level, where either complete control over the national heritage is exercised centrally (as in Greece, for instance) or the national body adopts a coordinating rather than a controlling role over local authorities to which powers are delegated (the situation largely applying in England).

The tradition in English-speaking countries, and those such as India which have been influenced by anglophone practices, is for a distinction to exist between the administration of the material heritage and other heritage institutions, such as universities and museums. Accordingly, while university departments of archaeology and history, local and regional museums and local authorities in England will communicate, coordinate and cooperate, they tend to see themselves – and accordingly tend to be treated – as quite separate institutions. This will also be reflected in legislative measures, which treat museums, universities and other cultural institutions separately from archaeology. Elsewhere – especially in European continental countries such as France, Denmark and Greece but also in Japan and Korea – museums are an integral part of archaeological and heritage administration, commanding and exercising much authority. In terms of overall effectiveness of heritage management as between one state and another these styles of organization probably make very little difference, but they are perhaps indicative of the different attitudes towards the physical heritage and the different expectations of its management that have yet to be properly explored.

By far the greatest amount of effective legislation in the heritage field is to be found at the level of the nation-state (Table 3.8). It is easy to underestimate how much such legislation exists and how wide the coverage is by different laws: it is always worth bearing in mind that every nation-state worldwide has at least some legislation relating specifically to its material heritage. In federal states, laws will be promulgated at both the federal and state or provincial level, the former often providing the model to be followed by individual states. In unitary states, the law at the national level will operate everywhere within that state.

While the specifics of legislation and administration will vary from country to country, certain trends are noticeable. There is a

Table 3.8 Archaeological laws at the national level

Territory	Level		Date	Title
USA	Federal		1906	Antiquities Act
			1966	National Historic Preservation Act
			1974	Archaeological and Historic Preservation Act
			1979	Archaeological Resources Protection Act
			1987	Abandoned Shipwreck Act
			1990	Native American Grave Protection and Repatriation Act
Australia	Federal		1975	Australian Heritage Commission Act
			1976	Historic Shipwrecks Act
			1984	Aboriginal and Torres Strait Islanders Heritage Protection Act
	State	ACT	1991	Land (Planning and Environment) Act
			1991	Heritage Objects Act
		NSW	1974	National Parks and Wildlife Act
			1977	Heritage Act
			1980	Historic Houses Act
		NT	1989	Aboriginal Sacred Sites Act
			1991	Heritage Conservation Act
		QLD	1992	Queensland Heritage Act
		SA	1978	South Australian Heritage Act
			1981	History Trust Act
			1988	Aboriginal Heritage Act
		TAS	1975	Aboriginal Relics Act
		VIC	1972	Archaeological and Aboriginal Relics Preservation Act
			1981	Historic Buildings Act
			1981	Historic Shipwrecks Act
		WA	1933	Lands Act
			1972	Aboriginal Heritage Act
			1973	Maritime Archaeology Act
			1990	Heritage of Western Australia Act
UK	National		1955	Inspection of Churches Measure
			1968	Pastoral Measure
			1969	Redundant Churches and Other Religious Buildings Act

Table 3.8 – *continued*

Territory	Level	Date	Title
UK	National	1973	Protection of Wrecks Act
(*continued*)		1979	Ancient Monuments and Archaeological Areas Act
		1983	National Heritage Act
		1986	Protection of Military Remains Act
		1990	Planning (Listed Buildings and Conservation Areas) Act
		1996	Treasure Act

marked tendency for nations, part of whose population is indigenous, to make a distinction between the legislation relating to their heritage and that of the majority. Accordingly, in Australia separate laws deal with the heritage of European incomers and that of Australia's Aboriginal peoples. Similarly, in the USA a specific piece of federal legislation governs the fate of the remains of native people; at the level of each state the decision will have been taken whether to treat the heritage of Native Americans as part of the general heritage or whether to separate it out. In many parts of the world colonized by Europeans, there has been a tendency to treat the indigenous population as part of 'nature'. Accordingly, indigenous North Americans have until recently been a subject of the Museum of Natural History in Washington; and the history of indigenous Africans has until very recently been excluded from the Cultural History Museum in Capetown, South Africa.

Although not necessarily typical of unitary states, heritage law in the UK comprises much more than only that relating obviously to archaeology and architecture. While National Heritage and Ancient Monuments laws cover archaeology and its administration, part of maritime law covers historic wrecks, ecclesiastical law governs Church property and laws relating to property and treasure govern portable antiquities. In addition, laws concerning the natural environment and its protection govern monuments and features as part of that environment; and bodies involved in agriculture, mining and quarrying or those providing amenities such as power, water and transport are charged with responsibility for components of the heritage on land they own and operate. In many countries, including the UK, laws relating to finance and taxation will make specific provision for heritage objects, as well as laws regulating the import and export trade, and this serves to emphasize the similarity of coverage heritage laws provide across the world. The main categories of portable objects, important public buildings, monuments, sites and landscapes (as outlined in Chapter 2) together with historic wrecks, military remains and – often – human remains tend to be those recognized and protected under all national heritage laws worldwide. This in turn reflects the strong measure of agreement globally as to what constitutes heritage, even though the world is wide and human culture is widely diverse across that world.

Functions and organizations

In the same way that heritage laws display a great similarity in terms of content across the world, so do the functions exercised by the organizations dedicated to managing the heritage. While organizations at the lowest level of the organizational hierarchy for heritage – frequently the local ones – have the specific task of actually managing individual components of the heritage and thus putting into practice the items on the list set out in Table 1.6, higher-level organizations take on the role of overseer and coordinator. In adopting such a role, international and national agencies share many of the same functions in respect of the heritage. Three of these universal functions in particular are worthy of further comment since they each reflect important aspects of the workings of archaeology and heritage management as fields of activity.

STANDARDS, REGULATION AND PROFESSIONALISM

High on the list of these universal functions of heritage agencies is the setting of appropriate standards for performance. This in turn derives from one of the functions many of them share (Tables 3.2 and 3.9) – that of encouraging, promoting and exchanging expertise, which in turn provides the basis on which they can offer advice to those who have operational responsibility for heritage matters. At the international level this can take the form of Charters, Recommendations and Conventions (which can be considered advice given to nation states on how to treat their

Table 3.9 Functions of national bodies

Parks Canada (www.parkscanada.pch.gc.ca)	On behalf of the people of Canada, to protect and present nationally significant examples of Canada's natural and cultural heritage and foster public understanding, appreciation and enjoyment in ways that ensure their ecological and commemorative integrity for present and future generations
Australian Heritage Commission (www.environment.gov.au/heritage/)	To give advice to the Minister, on matters relating to the national estate, including advice relating to: (i) action to identify, conserve, improve and present the national estate; and (ii) expenditure by the Commonwealth for the identification, conservation, improvement and presentation of the national estate; and (iii) the grant of financial or other assistance by the Commonwealth for the identification, conservation, improvement or presentation of the national estate; To encourage public interest in, and understanding of, issues relevant to the national estate; To identify places included in the national estate and to prepare a register of those places; To furnish advice and reports; To administer the National Estate Grants Program, being the program devised for the grant by the Commonwealth, in accordance with that Part, of financial assistance to the States and internal Territories and to approved bodies for expenditure on National Estate projects; To further training and education in fields related to the conservation, improvement and presentation of the national estate;

table continues

Table 3.9 – *continued*

	To make arrangements for the administration and control of places included in the national estate that are given or bequeathed to the Commission; To organize and engage in research and investigation necessary for the performance of its other functions.
English Heritage (National Heritage Act 1983, s. 33)	Duties: To secure the preservation of ancient monuments and historic buildings; To promote the preservation and enhancement of the character and appearance of conservation areas; To promote the public's enjoyment of, and advance their knowledge of, ancient monuments and historic buildings and their preservation. Functions: To provide educational facilities and services, instruction and information to the public in relation to ancient monuments, historic buildings and conservation areas; To give advice in relation to ancient monuments, historic buildings and conservation areas; To carry out, defray or contribute to the cost of research in relation to ancient monuments, historic buildings and conservation areas; Make and maintain records in relation to ancient monuments and historic buildings.

heritage), while at the national level it takes the form of the passage of laws. Chapter 4 will have more to say about laws in general and how they work on the heritage, but here it is worth emphasizing the role of laws in determining what can be considered as heritage. Laws – whether international or national – always closely define their object and, in the case of heritage laws, this often takes the form of a list of characteristics heritage objects must have. By setting such things down the laws not only describe the heritage but also go beyond this into prescribing what it shall be.

However, the regulatory influence such documents can give an organization also allows them to produce other forms of standard-setting documentation. For instance, Parks Canada publish as part of their website (http://parkscanada.pch.gc.ca/library/PC_Guiding_-Principles/) their *Cultural Resource Management Policy*, setting out the principles guiding their treatment of the historic places in their care. In the UK, English Heritage seek to guide the conduct of publicly funded archaeological work by encouraging a particular managerial approach (English Heritage, 1991). English Heritage were also responsible for producing the nationally applicable guidelines for local authorities on the treatment of archaeological sites under threat from development projects (DoE, 1990), and their application and effectiveness is monitored by them. The message of such products – whether international or national - is that of the particular expertise of the people responsible for them, which in turn encourages the professionalization of the discipline as a whole.

Other bodies take an equal interest in setting standards of appropriate performance in archaeology. These usually lack any legal power but nevertheless derive authority from the overall professionalization of the field encouraged by the emphasis placed on expertise and specialist knowledge by national and international heritage agencies. These professional associations are established to serve the interests of archaeologists themselves and often do more than merely offer standards of performance, by providing opportunities for archaeologists to meet and discuss matters of common interest at conferences and congresses. Membership of some such bodies may also indicate that a particular individual has achieved a certain level of expertise as an archaeologist and is therefore a suitable individual to undertake particular kinds of professional task. In contrast, some are primarily academic institutions, membership of which says little or nothing about the capacity of the individual. By offering codes of ethics or standards of performance, however, these bodies seek to confirm the expertise and professionalism of archaeologists as a whole. An overview of the statements of good practice produced by the bodies listed in Table 3.10 reveals a close

Table 3.10 Some professional bodies in archaeology

Territory	*Professional organization with ethics code*
Europe	European Association of Archaeologists (academic)
UK	Institute of Field Archaeologists
	Standing Conference of Archaeological Unit Managers
	Association of Local Government Archaeological Officers
USA	American Anthropological Association (academic)
	Society for American Archaeology (academic)
	Register of Professional Archaeologists

similarity of idea as to those to whom (or to which) archaeologists should consider themselves responsible (Table 3.11). This reflects not only the global nature of archaeology as a discipline, but also the ease with which aspects of archaeology related to heritage issues become accepted across the globe.

FUNDING AND THE CONTROL OF ARCHAEOLOGICAL WORK

The provision of funds for heritage preservation and other work is not much discussed in the literature of the field. In general, as a state-sponsored exercise, it is considered the role of government to provide the necessary resources and administrative framework for the work to be undertaken, and accordingly the effect of particular kinds of funding arrangements are not often considered. Like so much in the heritage field, this aspect of heritage activity is assumed to be simply a matter of pragmatics, a practical problem to be addressed locally in specific circumstances rather than a matter of

Table 3.11 Agents to whom archaeologists are deemed answerable

The public/society at large
Colleagues/the discipline of archaeology
The archaeological record (as evident today)
The past
Students
Sponsors/clients
Governments and laws

theoretical or philosophical concern. There are currently two main approaches to the control of archaeology and the provision of funds for archaeological work, however, with different implications for understanding archaeology and the heritage.

By far the most common is that of central regulation by state control, in which heritage objects are deemed to be the property and thus the responsibility of the nation state and its agencies. Under such a system, only those accredited by the state (frequently its employees) are entitled to conduct archaeological or conservation work. Accordingly, excavation by anyone else is commonly a criminal activity. In theory at least, all building and other work will cease when archaeological remains are encountered and state-employed archaeologists will move onto the site. In practice, however, limitations apply to this potentially draconian system. Small developments will be allowed to proceed unhindered, government-sponsored projects may also proceed without the interference of an archaeologist and, in many countries where such systems apply, lack of resources will result in incomplete coverage. Nevertheless, the ideal of such a system is a very powerful idea and dominates much thinking in the heritage field. It is the ideal assumed to exist by most international agencies, such as UNESCO, and very often those territories or areas not applying this approach can be thought to be deficient. Here, archaeology is a cost carried out of taxation levied on the entire community in whose service it is deemed to exist. It is archaeology (and indeed heritage) as bureaucracy (an issue to be discussed further in Chapter 4).

The alternative system, which applies mostly in anglophone countries such as the UK and the USA, is that of a partially privatized archaeology. This is essentially a private enterprise system under a measure of regulation by state and state-empowered authorities. In general there will be no limitation on who may carry out archaeological work, although professional bodies will seek to encourage the employment of those accredited by them. Excavation itself will most often be carried out as a result of the need to mitigate the damage of archaeological remains by development projects. In the USA material of 'scientific significance' may need to be retrieved or preserved; in the UK, the emphasis is theoretically upon preservation *in situ*, but frequently results in rescue excavation and so-called 'preservation by record'. Where development work reveals archaeological remains, the developer will be responsible for employing archaeologists to carry out the appropriate work, monitored by the local authority to ensure proper standards of recording. Here, archaeology is a cost levied on the developer, treating damage to the heritage as a form of pollution and applying the principle of 'the polluter pays' for restitution. This is archaeology (and indeed heritage) as enterprise, although never completely unregulated and much of the discussion of such systems turns upon issues of regulation and control rather than freedom of action.

INVENTORY

The process of recording the heritage is a key function of heritage agencies at every level of organization. The justification behind inventory is that no decision about the future of the heritage can be taken unless there is clear knowledge of what the heritage consists of. As mentioned above, it is one of the roles of laws in the field to determine what particular characteristics heritage objects and places must have. Accordingly, the task of inventory is to match objects and places with that list of legally approved characteristics. Table 1.3 set out the difference between the archaeological record, resource and heritage in this respect: whereas the archaeological record (the object of research activity) is identified by survey, the resource and heritage (the objects of management) are identified by a process of categorization. This involves in particular the matching of objects and places with the particular and predetermined attributes they need to have in order for them to be classed as heritage objects. Such inventories of 'approved' heritage objects exist at every level of heritage organization. The UNESCO World Heritage List promoted and managed by ICOMOS is an inventory of those sites and places considered by individual nation states to be of particular importance. Similarly, at the national level in every state of the world, certain sites are marked as being of particular importance or significance (an issue to be addressed in Chapter 6). However, in order that sites and places can be separated out as special, there also needs to be a general background inventory of all those things and places which fall into the 'heritage' category.

In the UK, this general inventory is referred to as the Sites and

Monuments Record (SMR), kept by the archaeologist employed by each county local authority. Ideally – although it is likely that none is entirely complete nor up to date – these records comprise the details of all monuments, find spots for antiquities, archaeological sites and sites where archaeological work has been conducted throughout the county. In addition to the SMRs, English Heritage has responsibility for the National Monuments Record, which acts as an index to the more detailed SMRs. Taken together they are a near-complete record of the nation's heritage (Aberg and Leech, 1992; Fraser, 1993). Elsewhere in Europe, reliance is generally placed upon a single national database (National Museum of Denmark, 1992). In federal states, such as Australia and the USA, responsibility for recording the heritage falls upon both federal and state agencies, often in collaboration with others, such as organizations representing indigenous peoples. Here, co-ordination will be carried out by one particular federal body – in the USA it is the National Park Service (Canouts, 1992) and in Australia it is the Australian Heritage Commission which keeps the records of the National Heritage Estate (www. cnvironment.gov.au/heritage).

In all cases of inventory, the emphasis is strongly placed upon the completeness and accuracy of the records held and the methods of recording applied. Further emphasis is also placed upon methods of retrieval of the information held and the uses to which it is put. To some extent these interrelate, especially with the increasing use – and planned use – of information technology and all are subject to the promotion of common standards (Thornes and Bold, 1998). These issues become of even greater importance where separately compiled sets of records are intended to be united to form a single overarching record. Here, the problems of coordinating record types and translation from one system to another become very evident and very important (National Museum of Denmark, 1992).

The museum as an institution

ICOM defines a museum as:

> a *non-profitmaking, permanent institution* in the service of society and of
> its development, [which is]
> *open to the public*, [and]

> which *acquires, conserves, researches, communicates, and exhibits* ...
> *material evidence* of man and his (*sic*) environment [for the purposes of
> study, education and enjoyment]. (ICOM, 1989, emphasis added)

Museums are, therefore, internationally recognized as permanent
(rather than temporary) institutions which are publicly accessible,
holding collections of material objects for recreational and academic
purposes. Accordingly, any institution that does not meet all of these
criteria is not a museum. In terms of these functions, the museum is a
unique type of institution. Museums play a part in archaeological and
heritage administration in many parts of the world and are formally
included in the heritage administrative hierarchy. Whereas all other
public heritage institutions – from the global to the local – may share
some of the museum's functions, none of them are required to be
open to the public in so doing. However, as discussed in Chapter 2,
the functions of the museum in relation to collections are also similar
to those of private owners. In locating the museum somewhere along
a continuum of 'publicness', therefore, the museum ranks very high
in terms of public access but relatively low in terms of other kinds of
behaviour as a 'public' institution.

Having said this, the functions of museums relating to collections
can be very similar to other kinds of heritage institution. Frequently
museums exist and are managed by virtue of national laws which
specifically provide for them. Inside the museum itself, collections
management, in particular, is not dissimilar to the function of
inventory, since it involves recording the content and condition of
the collection. Museums across the world are a repository of
expertise on many aspects of the material heritage and its
conservation. In interpreting the material they hold in their
collections and placing it on display, museums are very often the
most accessible entry people have to their past. Because of this, it is
often assumed that the prime function of the museum is to display
material for the public, and that this is – and has been – universally
recognized by the museum community. Many museum curators,
however, are much more interested in the material than in making it
publicly available.

In general, and in reality, the two most valued things in most
museums, from the point of view of their curators, are the reserve
collection (those materials held as part of the museum collection but

not put out on public display) and the museum curator. Visit almost any museum in any part of the world and you will find the reserve collection and the curator's office close together. What is more, it is likely that they will both be upstairs and towards the rear of the museum. This is reflected in requirements for museum design: 'Non public areas are best protected when they are separated from public areas by ... different levels. ... Artefact storerooms and vaults should be placed in the inner parts of the building' (Tillotson, 1977: 174). Treasured objects put on display will be deep in the museum, away from its public entrance, and safely kept in securely locked cases and cabinets. Thus, 'At the end of the second floor of the Museo Correr is a small room reserved for ... the great treasures of the collection' (Brawe, 1965: 7): this is as 'private' as can be managed in the public museum display space. Inevitably in the museum, the things least valued are in practice in the 'public' areas of the museum.

Museums in changing times

If – as some such as Fukayama (1992), Baudrillard (1981) and Walsh (1992) have argued – we live in a new age, that of the post-modern, then the essentially modern institution of the museum may need to adapt to new social and ideological conditions. The historian Hayden White (1973) has suggested four styles of story that historians may tell and these can be adapted for use by museums (Carman, 1996b):

- tragedy – in which the hero resists but is overcome by outside forces;
- comedy – in which the hero makes an accommodation with outside forces;
- romance – in which the hero overcomes the outside forces; and
- satire – in which the hero disengages from the fray to make sardonic comments from the side.

There is a sense in which all museums adopt a position of *ironic disengagement* by offering to tell stories about the world at all. However, the truer satirist is perhaps the commentator on the museum and indeed on heritage matters in general – such as the author of this book.

One possible approach to a changed world is for museums to seek to maintain the principles upon which many of our older museums were founded. These focus upon the collection of objects which are organized in a single rational structure of knowledge to form the basis of a public service (cf. Cannon-Brookes in Boylan, 1992: 81). These are the values defended in Wilson's (1989) discussion of the purpose and politics of the British Museum, where he was Director. In particular he emphasizes the public service role of the museum, the museum as a repository of expertise and the proper respect shown to the objects in its collections, all of which serve to support the institution as a great cultural benefit to the world at large. But, if indeed the world is changing into a new one – where the traditional values of the museum no longer hold good – such an approach represents increasing irrelevance. This is therefore inevitably a *tragic* response where the forces of change will sweep away or relegate to the unimportant institutions organized upon such lines.

A second possible response is to answer the charges made against museums that they are élitist and exclude large portions of the population they are meant to serve. In doing so, the museums may embrace the notion of 'multiple truths' and become, for example, 'ecomuseums' which focus on the construction of places as both physical locations in geographic space but also social spaces with a historic time dimension (Walsh, 1992: 160–4). They may also embrace the notion of 'cultural empowerment' and become truly local institutions. This may involve recruiting staff locally, encouraging community use of the museum space for non-museum activities, making the reserve collection available for public view, and organizing outreach activities to take the museum to people beyond its walls (Merriman, 1991: 132–9). The aim is to popularize the museum in the fullest sense and to use the techniques of the museum's rivals – amusement arcades, theme parks – to work for the museum as a visitor attraction. In defence of the principle of public service, other principles – a focus on the collection of objects and on single structures of knowledge – are compromised or abandoned in favour of new techniques, a focus on people rather than things and relative truth rather than absolute certainties. This is the *comic* response: an accommodation with the forces that threaten the survival of the museum as an institution.

A third response is neither to attempt to keep things the same nor to adjust to some new conditions while ignoring others, but to embrace the altered circumstances and create a new kind of museum for a new world. Such attempts are few and rare – possibly non-existent – in the West, but in areas where the idea of the museum itself is relatively new some exciting developments are taking place. In parts of West Africa the realization has developed that the museum is the repository of a 'traditional' 'past' culture which is still highly and presently active in the nearby marketplace. This is especially represented by the continuing use in the marketplace of 'traditional' objects and materials, examples of which are preserved for display in the museum. Accordingly, this has led to a blurring of the distinction between the 'closed' space of the museum and the 'open' space of the market, so that museum objects and tasks are taken out to the marketplace while market activities – such as traditional manufacturing activities – are invited into the museum space. Museum objects are thereby seen and experienced fully in their social context and the relevance of the museum collection becomes evident to the local community, since the museum ceases to be simply a space into which objects disappear once their useful life is over. This blurring of past and present, the traditional and the current, is the negation of the museum as we have come to know it; and it works by redefining the museum. The museum here ceases to be object-based and focuses instead on the social relations created and marked by the use of certain kinds of material culture; it ceases to be a distinct institution separated from everyday life and instead becomes an integral part of ongoing social practice. In doing so it abandons the principle of 'public service' in the usual narrow sense of 'providing access' in favour of a very active involvement in community life. This is the *romantic* response to changed circumstances: it faces the challenges of a new environment and overcomes them by redefining its own nature.

The museum and archaeology

In terms of practice, archaeology and the museum are two quite different entities. Archaeology is the study of the human past through its material remains. It is an academic pursuit largely – although not exclusively – carried out away from the public gaze: whether carried out as part of a state-sponsored or free-enterprise activity, the 'public' nature of archaeology refers more generally to funding and administrative arrangements (to be discussed further in Chapter 4). Nevertheless, in terms of academic purpose and a focus on material, archaeology and museums would appear to be connected and Crowther (1989: 44) has suggested that museums are not only 'well placed ... to reflect [the process of archaeological work] but to control it'. Pearce (1993: 232) suggests that, in relation to archaeology, museums have three functions: to manage archaeological material; to present this material; and to 'research into both the "archaeological" dimension of the material ... and into its cultural nature as one of the agents that has helped to create our present views about the past'. The third of these would correspond to Patrik's (1985) suggestion (mentioned in Chapter 1) that a post-processual 'textual' reading of archaeological material is more suited to the post-excavation phase of investigation. What such suggestions fail to recognize, however, is that archaeology is concerned primarily with the contextual relations between objects and features. Once located in a museum, these objects have been ripped from their original context and placed in another, quite different one: that of the collection (discussed in Chapter 2). This fact of the de- (or re-) contextualization of material in the museum separates the two fields quite widely.

They are further divided in their public natures. Archaeology is public in the sense of being at the public service; whereas the museum is public not only in that sense but also in opening its doors to the community at large. These are quite different senses of the concept 'public' and will be further developed in Chapter 4.

Further reading

International styles of archaeological and cultural resource management

Cleere, H. F. (ed.) (1984) *Approaches to the Archaeological Heritage*. Cambridge: Cambridge University Press.

Cleere, H. F. (ed.) (1989) *Archaeological Heritage Management in the Modern World*. London: Routledge.

AUSTRALIA AND NEW ZEALAND

McKinley, J. R. and Jones, R. (eds) (1979) *Archaeological Resource Management in Australia and Oceana*. Wellington, NZ: New Zealand Historic Places Trust.

Pearson, M. and Sullivan, S. (1995) *Looking after Heritage Places: The Basics of Heritage Planning for Managers, Landowners and Administrators*. Carlton, Victoria: University of Melbourne Press.

Smith, L. and Clarke, A. (eds) (1996) *Issues in Management Archaeology*. St Lucia, Qld: Anthropology Museum University of Queensland (= *Tempus: Archaeology and Material Culture Studies in Anthropology* 5).

BRITAIN

Cooper, M. A., Firth, A., Carman, J. and Wheatley, D. (eds) (1995) *Managing Archaeology*. London: Routledge.

Hunter, J. and Ralston, I. (eds) 1993/7. *Archaeological Resource Management in the UK: An Introduction*. Stroud: Sutton.

USA

McGimsey, C. and Davis, H. (eds) (1977) *The Management of Archaeological Resources: The Airlie House Report*. Washington, DC: Society for American Archaeology.

Schiffer, M. B. and Gummerman, G. J. (eds) (1977) *Conservation Archaeology: A Handbook for Cultural Resource Managers*. New York: Academic Press.

WEST AFRICA

Andah, B. W. (ed.) (1990) 'Cultural Resource Management: An African Dimension. Forum on Cultural Resource Management at the Conference in Honour of Professor Thurstan Shaw', *West African Journal of Archaeology* 20.

Ardouin, C. D. (ed.) (1997) *Museums and Archaeology in West Africa*. Oxford and Washington, DC: James Currey and Smithsonian Institution Press.

Law in AHM

Greenfield, J. (1995) *The Return of Cultural Treasures*. Cambridge: Cambridge University Press.
Pugh-Smith, J. and Samuels, J. (1996) *Archaeology in Law*. London: Sweet and Maxwell.

The museum

Edson, G. and Dean, D. (1994) *The Handbook for Museums*. London: Routledge.
Miles, R. and Zavala, L. (eds) (1994) *Towards the Museum of the Future: New European Perspectives*. London: Routledge.
Moore, K. (ed.) (1994) *Museum Management*. London: Routledge.
Pearce, S. (ed.) (1989) *Museum Studies in Material Culture*. Leicester: Leicester University Press.

Summary points

1. Organizations concerned with aspects of the heritage exist at all levels, from the global and regional, through the national to the local. These organizations usually operate as a system of hierarchies.
2. It is at the national level that much of the authority in heritage matters lies. Nation states have responsibility for complying with international law, and it is national law that determines the fate of most heritage objects. In federal states, federal laws and structures will often determine the shape of structures at the state or provincial level.
3. Despite wide diversity in structure and internal organization, the duties and functions of heritage agencies tend to be very similar across the world. These include regulating systems of heritage management under regimes of law, and the promotion of expertise. Inventory is a key function at all levels of heritage organization, from the global to the local.
4. Two main systems for regulating archaeological work apply across the world. One is archaeology as a state responsibility, carried out by employees of state agencies under public funding. The other is a system of free enterprise, where archaeology is

funded by developers under the principle of 'the polluter pays', regulated by official agencies.

5. Museums are a particular and distinct type of heritage institution. They may be seen either as entirely separate from archaeology or as an integral part of archaeological organization.

The reconstructed heritage

Plate 3.1 Newgrange neolithic chamber tomb, Boyne Valley, Ireland (after reconstruction in concrete)

Plate 3.2 'Bull Fresco' balcony, Knossos, Crete (built of concrete)

Plate 3.3 Iron Age roundhouse, Butser, Hampshire, England (built using original materials)

Plate 3.4 Anglo-Saxon buildings, West Stow, Suffolk, England (rebuilt using original materials on the exact sites of the originals)

Plate 3.5 Medieval buildings, Weald and Downland Museum, Sussex, England (removed from their original positions and rebuilt)

Plate 3.6 Replanted gardens, Hatfield House, Hertfordshire, England

Plate 3.7 Seventeenth-century house, Dorp Museum, Stellenbosch, South Africa

4 'Public' Archaeologies 1
Defining the Public

The material constituting the heritage, discussed in Chapter 2, is often considered to be 'public property', the institutions responsible for managing the heritage, discussed in Chapter 3, are 'public' institutions, and some such institutions – such as museums – are 'open to the public'. The particular sense of the term 'public' is not necessarily the same in each of these usages. Accordingly, the aim of this chapter is to examine what the term 'public' means in these contexts and, in particular, to separate out two meanings that are often confused and indeed conflated.

It is proper to do this because one of the alternative terms for archaeological heritage management –the main topic of this book - is 'Public Archaeology'. This term is not particularly well defined and is, indeed, increasingly used very broadly. For Schadla-Hall, it is 'any area of archaeological activity that interacted or had the potential to interact with the public' (Schadla-Hall, 1999: 147). A year later, Schadla-Hall's colleague Neil Ascherson defined it in two senses: as concerning 'the problems that arise when archaeology moves into the real world of economic conflict and political struggle ... [accordingly, it] is about ethics' (Ascherson, 2000: 2); and as the task of asking 'Who are those who define Heritage, and what do they get out of it?' (Ascherson, 2000: 3). It was important that these individuals define their object because both were justifying journal publications devoted to the issue: Schadla-Hall a special issue of the *European Journal of Archaeology* (volume 2.2, 1999) and Ascherson the first issue of the journal *Public Archaeology*. The areas addressed in both publications were wide, encompassing archaeology as an official, state-sponsored enterprise and also archaeologists' relations with individuals who are not themselves archaeologists.

Heritage in the public realm

There is a wide measure of agreement in the literature of AHM that archaeological remains and their treatment are a matter of 'public' concern. Accordingly, McGimsey's (1972) seminal text *Public Archaeology* argued the case for legislation to protect archaeological material on the basis that such material was inevitably a matter of public concern. This principle is the position from which AHM practitioners generally proceed: they act as the guardians of items representing a 'public good' (Fowler, 1984: 110) and of items preserved 'in the public interest' (Cleere, 1989: 10). What is not clear is from where this 'public interest' derives and why it is given such emphasis in AHM. Indeed, there is very little questioning of the nature of this 'public' concern and there have been few attempts to understand it by archaeologists and other students of heritage.

A limited and rather simplistic sense of the heritage as a 'public' phenomenon contrasts with that taken towards 'public' things in other disciplines, especially those with which AHM inevitably interacts in its concerns for the contemporary environment of archaeology, such as those I have listed elsewhere (Carman, 1996c: 175–8). In popular usage, the 'public figure' is rarely someone to whom the 'ordinary' individual has access and a sociologist of knowledge notes that 'the cleavage between the private and public spheres [of life] is a basic principle of modernity' (Berger, 1973: 104). In sociology there has long been a recognition that the public interest does not equate with direct access by individual members of the population but refers instead to a specific domain of social action (cf. Benn and Gaus, 1983a, b). Giddens (1984: 197) similarly remarked that a 'private sphere of "civil society" is ... in tension with ... the "public" sphere of the state'. In economics, the concept of 'public goods' is defined in terms of direct access by all members of a given community (Douglas, 1987: 22) but where such access will be destructive, this by no means excludes the possibility of the good's non-availability for use by individuals. These sociological and economic understandings that the 'public realm' of social life can in practice have nothing to do with actual people has been combined into a recognition of its strongly corporate nature, which carries an aura of 'otherworldly morality' (Douglas and Isherwood, 1979: 29).

While archaeologists, historians, anthropologists and others have sometimes universalized the division between public and private in order to provide convenient and useable analytical categories (e.g. Mehrabian, 1976; Thomson, 1977; Sassoon, 1987; Wilson, 1988; Helly and Reverby, 1992; Swanson, 1992; Turkel, 1992; Bold and Chaney, 1993), these realms as we understand and recognize them are entirely modern (Benn and Gaus, 1983b: 25). The public/private distinction always presupposes 'a secular society in which individuals confront each other in the context of a legal framework upheld by the state, the institutional embodiment of the public – everyone' (Benn and Gaus, 1983b: 25). The division first opened up during the later medieval period and early modern period (Backschieder and Dykstal, 1996), at the same time as land was appropriated for private use (cf. Way, 1997), as houses were divided into separate rooms (Johnson, 1993) and the nature of power and its exercise changed (Foucault, 1977). By the nineteenth century the two realms were clearly separate: '*public*, as opposed to *private*, is that which has no immediate relation to any specified person or persons, but may directly concern any member or members of the community, without distinction' (Sir George Cornewall Lewis in 1832, emphasis in original; quoted in Benn and Gaus, 1983a: 32). The 'public interest' as most commonly understood today represents the generalized good of 'the group as a corporate agent' (Benn and Gaus, 1983a: 39) and has become institutionalized and abstracted (Benn and Gaus, 1983a: 39–43) so that 'the public interest' is paramount over individual rights and is taken to represent the balancing of all such rights (Gavison, 1983). It is affirmed and reified by processes of 'social poetics' – forms of social performance related to styles of rhetoric whose purpose is to reify social institutions, such as the state and its bureaucracies, and thus to 'literalize' such necessary fictions as an iconic 'national character' (Herzfeld, 1997).

Archaeology as bureaucracy

This abstract, institutionalized and rhetorical understanding of things 'public' is applicable to the heritage as a phenomenon because it is as an abstracted, institutionalized and rhetorical phenomenon that the heritage gains its place as a concept (cf. Herzfeld, 1991). Herzfeld's work on Rethemnos – a historic town on the Greek island of Crete – establishes that the town 'does not only belong to its citizens. It is also part of a modern nation-state with a monumental conception of history' (Herzfeld, 1991: 5). This 'monumental time is calibrated in well-defined periods. [As t]he bureaucratic measure of history, it is no less *managed* than [other kinds of time]; but it has the power to conceal the props of its management and to insist on the rightness of its results' (Herzfeld, 1991: 6–9, emphasis in original). In such a view, the heritage as a whole consists of individual objects (as discussed here in Chapter 2), but as a category into which objects are put it displays attributes of the abstracted, institutionalized and rhetorical nature of modern society itself. Accordingly, the qualities of a heritage object – the 'amount' of heritage it represents – can be measured along the dimensions of the distinction between the 'public' and the 'private'. In institutional terms, these include the degree of public funding devoted to a particular activity, to what extent organizations concerned are public or private (issues raised in Chapter 3) and the degree of public accountability to which those organizations are subject (an issue to be returned to in Chapter 6). Where archaeology is largely funded as a state enterprise out of taxation, it is clearly a public activity; organizations involved will be completely public bodies and accountable to 'the public' through various forms of statutory and political control. Where funding derives from private sources – such as individual developers of land – it can be largely considered as 'public' because it will be carried out under systems of regulation frequently governed by laws and controlled to a greater or lesser extent by official agencies. It is the public nature of archaeology in this organizational sense which underlies McGimsey's claim that 'there is no such thing as a "private" archaeology [because] no individual may act in a manner such that the public right to knowledge of the past is unduly endangered or destroyed' (McGimsey, 1972: 2–5).

Other – and additional – measures of the difference between the 'public' and the 'private' have been noted by sociologists. Ruth Gavison (1983) lists the dimensions of 'publicness' as: being known, accessibility, ownership, control, accountability and effect and intimacy, while Benn and Gaus (1983b) reduce these to three only. For them, *access* (Benn and Gaus, 1983b: 7–9) incorporates being known, physical accessibility and the degree of intimacy one may achieve with the object. *Agency* (Benn and Gaus, 1983b: 9–10) concerns the powers exercisable in relation to the object, especially those of the public official whose authority may exceed that of the individual citizen but which are also tightly constrained by law. Accordingly, agency incorporates issues of accountability and effect. *Interest* (Benn and Gaus, 1983b: 10–11) represents a 'diverse cluster of rights of ownership and control'. These various dimensions of 'publicness' interact, cross-cut and compete to create and represent the complexity of heritage as a modern phenomenon. This is one reason why it is such a difficult issue to approach without over-simplification (cf. the reduction of 'heritage' to a 'looted' history [Lowenthal, 1996], a 'popular' history [Walsh, 1992] or a 'nationalist' history [Wright, 1985]).

Especially in relation to Benn and Gaus' (1983b, 9–10) dimension of *agency* we also enter the realm of bureaucracy. Albrow (1970: 87–105) lists the various understandings of this term by social scientists: as a system of rational organization; as organizational efficiency; as rule by officials; as a system of public administration; as administration (rather than rule) by officials; as the form of a particular kind of organization; and as a metaphor and model for modern society. As defined by Berger (1973), bureaucracy is to matters social as technology is to things mechanical: its purpose is to impose 'rational controls over the material universe' (Berger, 1973: 202). Blau (1956: 19) lists the attributes of a bureaucratic system as: specialization, a hierarchy of authority and a system of rules and impartiality. In developing such ideas, Berger points out that the bureaucrat typically displays limited competence which requires the capacity to refer other questions elsewhere for coverage by an appropriate but different agency (Berger, 1973: 46), akin to specialization. The bureaucracy is always orderly (Berger, 1973: 50), obeying a system of rules, demonstrating 'general and autonomous organisability' (Berger 1973, 53), such as in a hierarchy, which gives an impression of system predictability and consistency, equivalent to a 'general expectation of justice' (Berger, 1973: 52) and impartiality. The sum of all these qualities is a kind of 'moralised anonymity' (Berger, 1973: 53), akin to the 'accountability' required of public institutions (cf. Carnegie and Wolnizer, 1996).

The implications of organizing a particular area of life as a bureaucracy can be, among others: the reification of public life – and its separation from 'ordinary' private life – from the top down rather than the 'organic' emergence of a separate public sphere from everyday practice; the regulation of social relationships within paternalistic structures; and the monopolization of certain areas of social life by the state (cf. Herzfeld, 1992: 182). All of these can be seen in the universal structures established to govern the archaeological heritage, as outlined in Chapter 3. In global heritage management, internationally agreed agendas set the conditions under which national schemes of heritage management operate; in turn, national schemes determine the shape of provincial and local systems. Heritage institutions generally operate through systems of law and regulation rather than through the search for consensus and community control: where local autonomy is granted a role, this often needs to be through systems of representation authorized by legal mandate (Fourmile, 1996; Field et al., 2000) and such mandates often ignore subsidiary interests, such as that of women (Smith, 1995). By operating through such systems of regulation, in practice the state abrogates to itself the control of heritage materials (Smith and Campbell, 1998).

The creation of heritage in the public realm – the role of law

As suggested in Chapter 3 and here, the exemplary public institution in relation to the heritage – and especially archaeology – is that of law. As Henry Cleere (1989: 10) puts it '[the heritage] is governed by legislation'. It also 'depends for its very survival upon close interaction with the realm of law' (McGimsey and Davis, 1977: 9), exists in a 'legal context' (Fowler, 1982: 4), a 'legislative context' (Schiffer and Gumerman, 1977: 3–9) or against a 'legislative background' (Darvill, 1987: 32) and relies upon 'legal mandates [for its] intelligent management' (Adovaiso and Carlisle, 1988: 74). Cleere (1989: 10) and McGimsey (1972) justify legislative action on the grounds of 'public interest'. In particular, Cleere (1989: 10) uses the term 'governed' to explain and justify the management of the archaeological heritage 'in the public interest'. A historical introduction to the theme of AHM (Archaeological Heritage Management) emphasizes the importance of law in its creation: 'archaeological heritage management may be deemed to have begun with the Swedish Royal Proclamation of 1666, declaring all objects from antiquity to be the property of the Crown' (Cleere, 1989: 1). The theme of legislation also plays a large part in comparative and other studies in AHM (Cleere, 1984a; 1989; *Archaeologia Polona*, 2000; Hunter and Ralston, 1993; Cooper *et al.*, 1995). Nevertheless, very few studies have been done which seek to understand the precise role of law in relation to archaeology (although see also Firth 1993; 1995).

A common approach is to compare the legal systems of two or more countries, although the difficulties of doing so meaningfully are frequently underestimated. Such comparisons tend to be merely descriptive in content because of the inherent problems involved: they often reduce commentators to saying either (and only) 'here they do this, there they do that' or to setting up one system as superior to another in a superficial manner. To have a truly meaningful comparison it is necessary to take three factors into account: differences between legal systems; differences in the nature of the material record of the past; and differences in the traditions and historical development of archaeology. The first of these covers such things as the basic assumptions relating to the interests to be served by law, the degree of appropriate state control held to be applicable in an area, of the weight to be given to property laws or of the expected powers and duties of state and other agencies. All of these will differ between one territory and another or one legal system (e.g. Common or Roman) and another. The second concerns the kind of material governed by the legal regime: monuments of earth or stone may proliferate in one territory, requiring perhaps one form of physical treatment; and standing buildings perhaps requiring different treatment may proliferate in another; elsewhere, the archaeological record may consist entirely of fragile scatters of material with nothing monumental or built at all (matters touched upon in Chapter 2). The third factor to be taken into account concerns the understanding given to the purpose and focus of archaeological work within a territory which may differ from that of another: different research traditions may exist, as may differences in the degree of professional and public involvement. Somehow all of these factors will need to be reduced to having the same effect in order to effectively carry out comparisons between one body of law and another. If they cannot, then it is appropriate to focus on a single jurisdiction at a time.

An analysis of English law as it operates on archaeological material carried out between 1989 and 1993 (published as Carman, 1996c) suggested a threefold process was at work, involving sequential sub-processes of selection of material for coverage, its categorization into legal and administrative terms and a final phase of valuation. The final phase represented the ultimate purpose of the process of law, which was to mark archaeological material as culturally important. In many ways, however, the most complex sub-process and the most interesting was that of categorization (summarized in Table 4.1). The table enumerates the various legally defined categories into which archaeological remains may be placed and below is a list of the legally empowered institutions and organizations to which they can be allocated for treatment. Thereafter, the changes that the law recognizes may be made to such material are also listed. These changes are of two kinds: 'physical' alterations in the material (such as removing all or part of it, transporting it elsewhere or placing a protective barrier around it); and 'moral' changes to the way it is understood and considered (such as changes in authority over it, of ownership or of status). These sub-processes of the larger categorization process are sequential and consequent upon one another: first comes the legal categorization of the remains, then their consequent allocation to a particular institution. From this combination, certain consequences follow in terms of the range of physical or moral changes that may be made to it or from which it will be protected.

Table 4.1 The categorization phase of the legal process in England

Organization of terms	*Legal terms*
Categories	
Static features	Monument, ancient monument, scheduled monument, protected monument, protected wreck
Buildings	Listed building, historic building, ecclesiastical property, church
Movables	Treasure, prohibited goods, scheduled goods
Locations	Area of archaeological importance, conservation area, restricted area, prohibited area, controlled site, protected place
Ancillaries	Crown land, curtilage, easement
Consequences of categorization	
Institutions	
state	Crown, Board of Trade, Treasury, Valuation Office of the Inland Revenue, Secretary of State, Chancellor of the Duchy of Lancaster, Ministers
quasi-state	HBMCE (English Heritage), RCHME, NHMF, Coroner, finder, local authority, investigating authority, Church of England, Church Commissioners, Diocesan Synod, parochial church council, churchwardens, advisory committee for the care of churches, architect, statutory undertaker
independent	Redundant Churches Fund, Architectural Heritage Fund, person/body with special knowledge or interest, developer, owner, occupier, person with interest, limited owner
Physical changes	
by institutions	archaeological investigation, inspection, observation, archaeological examination, custody, sampling, excavation, power of entry, assistance, survey (verb), search, bore, boarding, seizure, protection, preservation, maintenance, safe-keeping, provision, educational facilities, public use
by others	damage, demolition, destruction, obliteration, tipping, depositing, obstruction, flooding, clearance, clearance operations, operations

Table 4.1 – *continued*

Organization of terms	*Legal terms*
	disturbing the ground, exempt operations, works, excepted works, execution (of works), alteration, extension, addition, affixing, deliberate inclusion, unauthorized interference, tampering, repair, unearthing, removal, salvage services, salvage operations, moving, exportation, conveyance (of prohibited goods), diving, (use of) metal detector, public access, public display
Moral changes	
by institutions	control, regulation, restricting use, superintendance, acquisition, gift, devise, purchase, ownership, agreement, trust, guardianship, scheme, right of way, disposal, knowledge, information, instruction, educational services, inquiries, guidance, advice, survey (noun), reports, records, recording, publishing, schedule of monuments, designation order, building preservation notice, scheduled monument consent, class order, planning permission, certificate of non-listing, certificate, licence, export licence, conditions, notice to excavate, operations notice, financial contribution, voluntary contribution, grant, loan (of money), repayment, investment, salvage, valuation, payment, compensation, penalty
by anyone	development, finding, hiding, danger, false statement/information/document, interest, public inspection, insurance, loan (of object), bequest, forfeit, defences

Such a system is common to most states which have laws concerning the archaeological heritage, although the specific categories and institutions will differ. The routes that individual items may follow are tightly constrained. Under English law nothing but a movable object discovered by a 'finder' may be designated by a Coroner (who has the appropriate authority) as 'Treasure' (not all movable objects will be eligible); once so designated, however, its ownership will pass to the Crown. A single Bronze Age barrow, by contrast, cannot be categorized as anything other than a 'monument': once so designated, it becomes the joint responsibility of a number of agencies for various aspects of its treatment, including an archaeological unit or society for its survey and recording, English Heritage or the local authority for its preservation and management, a developer for its possible destruction, and so on. It may be further categorized as a 'scheduled monument' protected by law from damage and will thereby, under the law, gain the further status of 'ancient' and 'protected monument' and may be taken into care under 'guardianship' arrangements in which case it will also gain this extra status and be accorded appropriate treatment, such as the provision of public access for site visitors. An old building constructed and used for religious worship is the responsibility of Church authorities, their agents and specialist advisors, such as architects, but not of other agencies, such as English Heritage or a local authority. A historic wreck is the responsibility of an appropriate officer of the Board of Trade and is capable of designation as a 'protected wreck', in which case its site is a 'restricted area' protected from salvage operations (themselves a creation of and subject to legal regulation) (Carman, 1996c: 193–223).

'Public interest' and the general public: a conflict

This complex and bureaucratic manner of treating the archaeological heritage under law is highly codified and structured. It mirrors the kind of 'social poetics' exhibited by a bureaucracy, whereby the rhetoric of bureaucratic pettiness is 'evidence of ... political clout', that is of continuing importance (Herzfeld, 1997: 163). The 'rhetoric' of English law displayed here as it relates to the archaeological heritage, exemplified in its processes of categorization and consequent treatments, is one of the importance of that heritage. In order to underline this, agencies have been created that carry specific responsibilities for the heritage with the endorsement of law. Each category of heritage can only travel a limited number of routes through the legal categorization process, each step limiting the further options for different treatments and categorization. At each stage of the legal process it is further abstracted and reified, drawn into the institutionalized structure of the bureaucratized state, becoming an increasingly 'rhetoricized' phenomenon. There is no longer any direct connection with people: the public status of the heritage as a category is that of legislative and bureaucratic authority, divorced from the everyday and the ordinary. It is as reified and abstracted as the concept of 'law' itself, or of 'the state', as a social and political institution. It exists somewhere apart: it has become something marked as being very special and as 'public property'.

One of the things that is interesting, however, is that this public interest in the heritage as an institution does not generally extend to the public at large. Most of the available legal and bureaucratic arrangements for treating various types of heritage object (as outlined in Chapter 2) do not include provision for public access. As outlined in Chapter 3, only in the case of museums is public access a prerequisite and in 1990 a legal case in England made the point even more powerfully. The discovery in London of the extensive remains of Shakespeare's first custom-built theatre *The Rose* became something of a *cause célèbre* when it became clear that the relevant official of the government was not going to arrange for these nationally important remains to be given legal protection. Efforts to force the scheduling of the site by a group of concerned individuals led to a series of court hearings. After hearing all the relevant arguments, the judge ruled, first, that the official had absolute discretion in the matter of scheduling so long as the proper procedures were followed; and, second, that in any case the individuals bringing the action did 'not have sufficient interest [in the decision whether to schedule or not] to entitle [them] to' go to court (quoted in Carman, 1996c: 147). In other words, the protection of historic structures and remains in the public interest does not at all imply that individual members of the public are entitled to act upon that interest: the public interest here is a general one that does not attach to individuals but only to the agencies set up to administer those historic structures and remains. (For a fuller discussion of this see Carman, 1996c: 146–8; and for the full story of *The Rose* theatre see Biddle, 1989; Orrell and Gurr, 1989; Wainwright, 1989b; and Gurr, 1994.)

It is unlikely that this English example is unique to that country: since heritage management systems are (as discussed in Chapter 3) broadly similar across the world, it follows that the notions of 'public interest' applied will also be similar. Where remains and monuments are given protection under legal and bureaucratic arrangements, there is frequently no provision for access by individual members of the public. Accordingly, the individuals who constitute that public can claim no right of access or a direct involvement with decision-making regarding those remains or monuments. In this manner, the concept of 'public interest' in global systems of heritage management contradicts and is directly in conflict with the actual public on whose behalf it claims to act.

The public as other people

The conventional argument applied in AHM is that 'the past [inevitably and by right] belongs to all' (Merriman, 1991: 1), but this does not lead logically to the conclusion that all humans have an interest in the preservation of archaeological remains. Instead, there is the perceived need to create such an interest by various means and this is recognized by writers in the AHM field: both McGimsey (1972) and Cleere (1984b, 61–2; 1984c: 128) press the case for programmes of public education and McGimsey (1984) offers advice as to how to 'sell' archaeology to non-archaeologists. Accordingly, the literature of heritage management abounds with a limited concern with 'the public' as groups of people: common classifications include people as visitors, as tourists, as sources of revenue and capital funding, as audiences and as customers (Cleere, 1989: 10; Merriman, 1991; Walsh, 1992; Boniface and Fowler, 1993; Carman, 1995). There has been, however, surprisingly little work done on the specifics of identifying and understanding the archaeological public.

Categorizing the public

Drawing on his personal experience in the USA and 'common sense' categories, McManamon (1991) chose to divide the public in the USA into five main groups, most of which could be considered to have correlates in every other part of the globe. These are: the general public (at large); students and teachers (i.e. those in education); Members of Congress and the Executive Branch (legislators); government attorneys, managers and archaeologists (professionals); and Native Americans (indigenous peoples). Referring to wider studies of the general public and their attitudes to science in the USA and elsewhere, he suggests that only up to 5 per cent of the US population can be considered 'archaeologically literate' – that is, well informed about archaeology and what archaeologists do. A further 25 per cent can be considered informed about and interested in scientific topics generally, including archaeology. The remaining 70 per cent are not at all well informed on scientific topics and are largely uninterested in learning more, but they also show themselves to be generally supportive of scientific endeavours, including archaeology (McManamon, 1991: 123). These categories are clearly not intended to be exclusive: the public at large must also include the other four categories, and there is no reason why a professional archaeologist in government service may not also be a student or teacher, a manager or a Native American, although McManamon treats them as quite distinct. All of the categories save that of Native American will have a correlate in any other country of the world, since they can all be expected to have educators and students, legislators and government employees. Not all countries have an indigenous population that can be considered in some way separate from the majority dominant population: in European countries the dominant population will generally be considered as the indigenous population and it is more recent incomers who will be in the minority. In this context, it is interesting that McManamon does not distinguish African–Americans whose interest in archaeology and the past may be considered to be different from that of the dominant European–American population. Although the differences between the situation and status of African–Americans in the USA and incomer populations in Europe are many, such a distinction would allow an extension of McManamon's categories beyond the confines of the USA, at least in broad terms.

A more recent and much more scientific survey of mostly well-educated and middle-aged European–Canadians in British Columbia, Canada (Pokotylo and Guppy, 1999), established that over 80 per cent of respondents had 'accurate' or 'reasonable' understandings of archaeological purposes and practices. By contrast, very few were aware that the bulk of archaeological work was carried out by consultants doing commercially sponsored CRM (Cultural Resource Management) work rather than by government or university-based researchers. There was large-scale uncertainty about certain aspects – such as the antiquity of human occupation in the region, the accessibility and range of information about archaeology available, how interesting archaeology was to the respondent personally and the details of legislation relating to archaeological preservation. In contrast to this, there was wide-spread agreement that archaeology was of importance in the contemporary world, whether this was prehistoric, historic or classical archaeology. In identifying specific areas in which archaeology was of contemporary relevance, the majority of responses focused on issues of aboriginal land claims and rights, land and resource development, conservation of heritage sites, the stewardship and repatriation of cultural property and vandalism, looting and the antiquities trade. This last finding is somewhat at odds with the finding that few respondents, on being asked to define archaeology, equated the field with an interest in aboriginal concerns or peoples.

A concern with planning issues led to work by Ennen (2000) in Holland, which established the existence of three types of attitude towards living in a historic city centre. The 'connoisseurs' are drawn to the cultural heritage and appreciate its existence around them: these are the kind of people who will seek out a historic building as a home. The 'take-it-or-leavers' are often those forced by circumstance to live in the city centre but who have come to terms with it and feel comfortable there, so that when their environment is threatened by change they react against it. The 'rejecters' emphasize the disadvantages of living in a city centre, even though (for reasons other than that of its heritage value, such as proximity to employ-ment) they may have chosen to live there: for them the heritage is an obstacle to progressive change. Such distinctions also inform Szacka's (1972) work in Poland. This focused exclusively upon university-educated people and identified two attitudes to the past: the 'historicist' orientation, one in which time is linear and a clear continuity and connection between past and present is evident; and the 'escapist' orientation, one which takes the form of a desire to live in some part of time other than the present. Such work as this is useful because it opens up the possibility of understanding different attitudes to the past held by different kinds of people. Rather than a generalized 'gloss' treating the population as a single mass, it invites us to consider the different audiences for archaeology and how archaeology can serve them, if at all.

People's attitudes to the past

Drawing upon such ideas as these, by far the most widespread study of attitudes to the past so far has been carried out in Britain. Merriman's (1991) large-scale postal survey of public attitudes to the past established one connection between certain groups of people and the kind of knowledge of the past generated by archaeology and a separate connection between a very different – much more personal, family-oriented – past and other groups of people. The survey drew on ways of categorizing people commonly used in social research in particular, in terms of relative wealth and social position. Accordingly, by the application of certain measures, people were placed into categories: 'high status' – those who are relatively wealthy with high educational attainment; 'middle status' – those with moderate wealth and average educational attainment; and 'low status' – those who are relatively poor with low educational attainment. It also compared people in terms of their relations to heritage sites and museums, as 'frequent', 'regular', 'occasional', 'rare' or 'non-' visitors to such places. These categories were to some extent correlated: frequent visitors tended to be high-status people as defined while rare and non-visitors tended to be low-status people as defined (Merriman, 1989; Merriman, 1991, 51). These categorizations then allowed the attitudes towards museums and heritage places held by different respondents to be analysed.

Perhaps the most important single finding was that of the level of value of knowing about the past indicated by the majority of respondents. Regardless of factors such as age or social status, over 68 per cent of all classes of respondent agreed that the past was worth knowing about (Merriman, 1991: 23). Further results, however, showed clear differences between categories of people in terms of the kind of knowing about the past they valued. Frequent visitors showed a preference for world and British history over more local and family pasts; by contrast, rare and non-visitors placed greater value on family and local history. Similarly, high-status people showed a preference for British and world history and those of low status a greater interest in family and national history (Merriman, 1991, 128). Frequent and regular visitors to museums were more likely to compare a museum to a library than to some other kind of structure; for occasional, rare and non-visitors, the most common comparison was with a monument to the dead, although they too chose a library as the most common second choice. All categories agreed on a religious building or school coming third. Few thought of museums as similar to community centres or department stores (Merriman, 1991: 62).

Out of these differences, Merriman constructs the distinction between 'a personal past' and 'the impersonal heritage' (Merriman, 1991: 129–30). The former is the sense of the past 'experienced in personal terms [such as] personal memories and family histories' and it may have no 'tangible manifestations[, although constituting] a more vivid experience of the past than any number of museum visits' (Merriman, 1991: 129). The latter is that sense of the past as something separate and detached, created by professionals and, most frequently, the kind presented in museums and other forms of display. These are the issues to be taken up in Chapter 5.

Further reading

Archaeology as a state-sponsored activity

Herzfeld, M. (1991) *A Place in History: Social and Monumental Time in a Cretan Town*. Princeton, NJ, and Oxford: Princeton University Press.
McGimsey, C. R. (1972) *Public Archaeology*. New York: Seminar Books.

Texts on bureaucracy and the public–private division

Albrow, M. (1970) *Bureaucracy*. London: Pall Mall Press.
Benn, S. I. and Gaus, G. F. (eds) (1983) *Public and Private in Social Life*. London: Croom Helm.

Berger, P. (1973) *The Homeless Mind*. London: Penguin.

Blau, P. M. (1956) *Bureaucracy in Modern Society*. New York: Random House.

Herzfeld, M. (1992) *The Social Production of Indifference: Exploring the Symbolic Roots of Western Bureaucracy*. Chicago: University of Chicago Press.

The public

Ennen, E. (2000) 'The meaning of heritage according to connoisseurs, rejecters and take-it-or-leavers in historic city centres: two Dutch cities experienced', *International Journal of Heritage Studies* **6** (4): 331–50.

McManamon, F. P. (1991) 'The many publics for archaeology', *American Antiquity* 56: 121–30.

Merriman, N. (1991) *Beyond the Glass Case: The Public, Museums and Heritage in Britain*. London: Leicester University Press.

Pokotylo, D. and Guppy, N. (1999) 'Public opinion and archaeological heritage: views from outside the profession', *American Antiquity* **64** (3): 400–16.

Summary points

1. The concept of 'public' as applied to archaeology is rarely subject to investigation or definition. The term is used in more than one sense and different meanings can often be conflated. This not only creates confusion, but can also mask the way in which archaeology is actually done and prevent deeper questioning of its aims and effects.

2. Archaeology 'in the public interest' is an archaeology carried out as an activity in an 'abstracted' and institutionalized 'public realm'. In such a sense, there can be no 'private' archaeology.

3. Archaeology in the public realm is a bureaucratic activity, established and regulated by systems of law. Such arrangements can deny real access to the past to 'the public', the term used here in the sense of the other human beings for whom archaeologists work.

4. Although the duty of an archaeologist to the public is widely

asserted, very little has been done by archaeologists to identify precisely who or what constitutes that public. The majority of efforts in this direction have inevitably been based upon assumptions untested by research.

5. The most detailed research into public attitudes to the past was conducted in Britain. It established the widespread interest in the past held by the majority of the population. It also identified two kinds of attitudes to the past held by different kinds of people. One was a preference for the kind of 'abstracted' and impersonal past usually offered by professional archaeologists and historians and by presentations in museums. The other was for a more personal, family-oriented past.

Heritage in the townscape

Plate 4.1 Nineteenth-century canal, England

Plate 4.2 Medieval city walls, Southampton, England

Plate 4.3 Seventeenth-century 'Blue' Mosque, Istanbul, Turkey

Plate 4.4 Roman aqueduct, Istanbul, Turkey

Plate 4.5 'Blockhouse', Stellenbosch, South Africa

5 'Public' Archaeologies 2
Engaging with the Public

Merriman's (1991: 62) finding that a large sector of the public find traditional and 'official' museum presentations more easily comparable to mausolea than anything else (as mentioned in Chapter 4) raises questions as to the manner in which archaeologists communicate with the public at large about our work. Accordingly, this chapter will continue the theme of our relations with the public by examining the various ways in which the work of archaeologists is made available to others and the relationships between archaeologists and other groups of people. This is the area which most archaeologists – and indeed others – are likely to consider as constituting a 'public archaeology', even though this term also covers a range of other fields covered in this book, including archaeology as a set of bureaucratic practices (discussed in Chapters 3 and 4).

This particular field is very much an area of practice and it is therefore no accident that this chapter, as well as drawing on the literature of applied public archaeology, draws heavily on the author's own experience, both as communicator with the public and as a member of that public. Public archaeology is also an area the literature of which is dominated by case studies and it is, therefore, also no accident that much of this chapter is structured as a series of informative case studies. In part, this structure simply reflects the standard approach to considerations of engaging with non-archaeological 'others', but it also serves to emphasize how little truly critical literature there is on these matters. Individual case studies very often represent the discourse of 'should', so often used in writing on AHM, since they serve to promote particular ways of communicating about archaeology and the past. Others are purely descriptive, but few take a broader perspective to consider general trends or the consequences of particular ways of talking to others, either to archaeology or to those others (for a rare exception to this rule, see Potter, 1994).

It is also worth noting that the kinds of public archaeology one may expect to encounter will vary from country to country. While this chapter uses examples from a number of different parts of the world, it is useful to bear territorial differences of 'style' in mind as they become evident: a commonly applied global set of public archaeology practices is not yet in existence, if indeed it is possible at all. It is also valuable to bear in mind the distinction between different 'public' archaeologies discussed in Chapter 4. For many, interaction with the public in the form of 'telling' them about their past is an integral part – and follows from – a bureaucratic style of public archaeology (McManamon, 2000; Heath, 1997; Hoffman, 1997). For others, dealing directly with other people is at odds with a bureaucratic archaeology, and serves to undermine and subvert it (cf. Leone and Potter, 1992; Leone *et al.*, 1987; Faulkner 2000). Beyond this is a growing realization that it is not necessarily the task of archaeologists to offer themselves as leaders and teachers, but to serve a particular public as it wishes to be served (Davidson *et al.*, 1995; McDavid and Babson 1997; Swidler *et al.*, 1997).

The presenting institution

Coming from the perspective of the museum as an institution (see Chapter 3), Belcher (1991) conveniently outlines the various kinds of displays that are possible in terms of the form they take and the purposes and styles they may represent (Tables 5.1 and 5.2). All of these forms and styles can be extended to other types of presentation.

A *temporary* display is any display that is put up by the institution for a known period of time and which will be replaced by another after that time has expired. A *permanent* display may also have an effective time limit to its duration but can be expected to be part of the museum's core displays and to have a significantly

Table 5.1 Forms of display

Temporary
Permanent
Loan
Special – e.g. 'blockbuster'
Travelling/circulating/touring
Portable
Mobile

Source: Belcher, 1991

longer life than a temporary one. A *loan* exhibition is one brought in from outside the displaying institution. A *special* exhibition is one that will be held very exceptionally, such as an exhibition of items collected from other institutions or for which visitors may be expected to pay an entry charge, especially if the norm at the host institution is for free entry. A *travelling, circulating* or *touring* exhibition is one made to be displayed at other locations: it will become a loan exhibition when mounted. A *portable* exhibition is one to be taken by museum staff out to non-museum places, such as fairs and other events. A *mobile* exhibition is an exhibition that travels around in and of itself, by being permanently housed in a van or bus. It will be evident that particular forms are not mutually exclusive: an exhibition may be both permanent and mobile or temporary and loan. It is also clear that these forms concern only the physical structure of the exhibition, which may or not reflect any given purpose or aim, and may be chosen for purely contingent and practical reasons: they say nothing about its audience or the message it hopes to deliver.

Styles of display specifically relate to the purpose and objective of mounting the display: they directly concern the outcome that the exhibition hopes to achieve. Some exhibitions are at root about the material on display and – while also seeking a particular outcome in terms of visitor response – are more concerned with the proper ordering of that material than with the proper ordering of visitors: these are 'object-centred' displays. A *systematic* display seeks to place similar kinds of object in relation to one another: whether in terms of some developmental sequence, such as from simpler to

Table 5.2 Purposes and styles of display

Visitor-centred	Object-centred
Didactic/educational	Systematic
Entertaining	Thematic
Emotive	Participatory
– aesthetic	
– evocative/romantic	
Responsive	
– to viewer's presence	
Interactive	
– with visitor's wishes	

Source: Belcher, 1991

more complex (however defined), or in chronological sequence. A *thematic* display will place together objects that are to be found or used in groups or as assemblages; they may be ordered in terms of functional utility or ritual association, for example. A *participatory* display is one in which visitors are encouraged to take part – either by visitors providing the objects to be put on show or by handling them and talking about them.

Although involving visitors very directly, a participatory exhibition is not itself 'visitor-centred', which is at root concerned with the effect of the exhibition on visitors rather than with specific content. A *didactic* or *educational* exhibition is one that actively draws the visitor to learn something in particular, whether about a period of the past, the work of the museum or of archaeologists or about particular kinds of objects. The exhibition planned as *entertainment* is not necessarily designed to educate or inform, although there is no reason why education cannot also be entertaining. So long as the visitor is educated or entertained or both, the exhibition has served its purpose: in this way, both styles are a one-way projection of ideas onto the visitor. The *emotive* exhibition seeks a return from the visitor, in the form of some kind of emotional response: an appreciation of the beauty of art objects, for example, perhaps horror or anger at an exhibition concerning the Holocaust or possibly nostalgia at an exhibition of photographs of local people and places which are now gone. A *responsive* exhibit

Table 5.3 Archaeological messages for the public

A local focus: archaeology is about local pasts
The value of archaeological resources
The need for care in study and conservation
The archaeological resource as non-renewable
The distinction between scientific archaeology and looting

Source: After McManamon 2000: 13–14

is one that reacts to the visitor's presence: triggered perhaps by electronic detection devices, doors may open to reveal exhibits or television screens come to life to show video sequences. An *interactive* exhibition is one in which the visitor is effectively made part of the exhibit: by selecting various routes through the information and other resources provided, he or she may construct their own understanding of the material on display (as discussed by Walsh, 1992: 167–70; 1995).

Taking a more explicitly archaeological and non-museum perspective, McManamon (2000) urges archaeologists to direct clear messages at particular publics. He also wishes the public at large to acquire knowledge of the various kinds of value the archaeological past can have: especially its associative and commemorative value and educational and information value (for more on value generally see Chapter 6). Accordingly he argues for particular kinds of messages to be directed at the archaeological public (as set out in Table 5.3) and for the adoption of a particular set of guidelines on doing so (set out in Table 5.4) (McManamon, 2000: 13–15).

When ideological conditions change: the case of South Africa

The general principles upon which public interpretation is usually based have been established in advance of actually providing public access. The principles have stayed in place because – although much learning has taken place by both presenters and their public – the circumstances within which this communication take place have been considered to have remained largely unaltered. But the world

Table 5.4 Guidance for communicating with publics

Find a hook
Tell a story
Include yourself
Avoid jargon
Talk to a single individual
Names are important
Determine the data you need
Present the data visually
Emphasize theory and methods
Always think 'audience'

Source: McManamon 2000: 15 (after Allen, 1995)

never stays exactly the same for very long, and changes can have a major effect upon the institutions of heritage and upon styles of public presentation.

Post-apartheid South Africa (Van Zyl Slabbert, 1992; van Vuuren, 1991; Woods, 2000) is perhaps a good laboratory for examining how the presentation of the past needs to adapt when its ideological context changes very suddenly. Traditionally in South Africa, the Black majority population were denied full citizenship rights, civil rights and indeed basic human rights. The legitimacy of Whites-only minority rule was supported upon the division of the South African population into distinct racial groups: Afrikaners (Whites of Dutch or French descent); British South Africans (Whites of British descent); Cape Muslims (the descendants of Asians brought to South Africa as slaves or servants during British rule); 'Cape Coloureds' (the descendants of those born of mixed White and Black parentage); and Blacks (a generic term covering all of South Africa's Black population). It was further supported upon a construction of the past which had the ancestors of the majority Black population arriving after Europeans (for a convenient summary of this vision of the South African past, see Morris, 1965: 17–39).

The end of apartheid from 1989, the adoption of a new constitution and the election of governments by the entire adult population has required a change in how South Africa understands

123

its past. This is partly reflected in its flag, which contains all the colours found in all South Africa's previous flags – whether under Dutch, British or Afrikaner rule – which mean it can be read in a number of different ways:

- as symbolic of *struggle* where the black area stands for South Africa's indigenous peoples, the white for European colonizers, the red for blood, the gold for the gold in the ground (and for wealth generally), the green for the land and the blue for the sea and sky;
- for the *completion of history* since all these colours also come from South Africa's previous flags: red, white and blue from the Dutch and British; black, gold and white from the Afrikaner Republic; and green, gold and black for the African National Congress which oversaw the collapse of apartheid;
- and for new-found national *unity* in the way in which all these colours flow together into a single stream.

Two dominant discourses are evident in the South African presentations of its past. One of these concerns issues of diversity and the separateness of South Africa's peoples. At historical places such as Stellenbosch – founded in the seventeenth century, the start-point of the 'Great Trek' inland by Afrikaners seeking to throw off British constraints in the early nineteenth century and home to the largest Africaans-speaking university in the country – much is made of the distinctive architecture called 'Cape Dutch'. Here, much effort is put into promoting an image of peaceful co-existence between Europeans and the indigenous population. The now-empty 'Blockhouse' occupying the centre of the town's main green space is presented as a 'store' for (largely unused) weapons; the fact that it would serve equally well as a fortress in times of conflict is glossed over. Also in Stellenbosch, the Dorp (or 'Town') Museum is a fine example of a Scandinavian-style open-air folk museum, comprising a number of buildings from the settlement's history, all *in situ*. From a late-seventeenth-century house – not dissimilar in style to indigenous vernacular building styles – through increasing Europeanization in the eighteenth and nine-teenth centuries to the twentieth, the story told is one of progress and the triumph of European civilization. In the museums of Cape

Town, South Africa's capital city, the division has always been maintained between reserving 'cultural' history for the non-indigenous population and a separate one for the Black population, whose history and ethnography were reserved for the National Museum, which is devoted to natural history. The Cultural History Museum itself has until very recently been entirely devoted to White history: current efforts to be more inclusive include sections on the native populations of the Cape region and their interaction – both violent and peaceful – with incoming Europeans and, in 1998 and 1999, an exhibition was devoted to the new national flag and its different contexts of use. Elsewhere, the 'Cape Muslims' have a museum devoted to their history in the shape of the Bo Kaap Museum, representing a 'typical' Cape Muslim house from the nineteenth century, and South Africa's Jewish population has its own museum in a converted synagogue. In the National Museum, displays representing the ways of life of the indigenous peoples have been enhanced by the inclusion of photographs of modern representatives of the Black population, emphasizing their fully modern and educated status.

The second discourse – never entirely absent from South Africa but nevertheless coming particularly to the fore in the new political and social conditions – is that concerning unity. One of the inevitable legacies of apartheid is pain, especially the pain of loss: for many, lost loved ones killed in the violence attending apartheid's overthrow; lost years in prison; lost homes and ways of life; for others again, loss of the secure sense of superiority, position and status apartheid provided. Robben Island – once a mountain before the seas rose, then a desert island, then from the fifteenth century a whaling station, from the eighteenth century a leper colony, then in the nineteenth and twentieth centuries a prison and military site – is now a museum recording all these aspects of its history (Clark, forthcoming). Organized tours are in two parts: a coach tour around the island showing important places in its various histories; and a walking tour through the former high-security prison where leaders of the anti-apartheid movement were held for many years in custody. Guides to the museum are chosen from among former guards or former political prisoners: accordingly, what is encountered is not a detached and distanced account of '*the* past' but a personalized perspective on a life as lived. Although focusing upon events and experiences that most of us would find too appalling to bear, it is also an encounter with hope for the future, emphasizing forgiveness and a willingness to put the past in its place. And as the tour continues, it ceases to be a 'one-way' presentation of experience, but – as guide and visitors become more familiar with one another – it becomes much more of a two-way exchange and, once beyond simple questions and answers, a conversation.

This 'conversational' aspect - an idea also present in the work of Carol McDavid and her colleagues (see below) - is also present at the District Six Museum, a collection of temporary displays housed in a church at the heart of the now-destroyed District Six area of Capetown (www.districtsix.co.za; Tunbridge and Ashworth, 1996: 223–62; Ballantyne and Uzzell, 1993; Uzzell, 1998: 167–8). There are few artefacts on display here: those that are to be seen were rescued from destroyed houses and are placed in small glass cases, replicating the physical relationships they had when the house was standing. The central feature of the museum is a huge map of District Six, taking up most of the floor so that it is almost impossible not to 'walk' the streets. On this map former residents write their memories of living in the area: 'this was my uncle's shop'; 'here is where we played as children'. On the wall hangs an enormous white cotton sheet, on which visitors and former residents alike are encouraged to mark their presence by writing their name and a few words. Former residents of the area are always present, sitting and drinking tea, maybe watching a video recording of a past event and noting those present on screen and absent now. They are happy to talk to visitors, indeed insist on doing so. They talk of what life was like before the area – which was mixed racially and socially, with a vibrant cultural life – was razed and its people forcibly moved to other parts of South Africa, of life under the apartheid regime and of hopes for the present and future. There are no plans to recreate District Six: its physical fabric was used to construct the Victoria Wharf tourist area and it may be left as an empty zone in memory of what was once there and what people – and governments – can do to other people.

Like Robben Island Prison, the District Six Museum is not a presentation of the past but an exercise in providing a topic of conversation through which strangers can meet and communicate. Unlike Stellenbosch, the Cultural History Museum, or sites such as Barquisimeto Museum, Flag Fen or even Annapolis (all to be discussed below) they involve visitors in the process of engaging with the past rather than being told about it. Here, visitors are as much a part of the interpretation as the presenters.

The archaeologist as teacher

Traditionally, at least in the West, archaeologists and others 'tell' people about the past: that is, we decide what we shall communicate about our work and how and prefer our audiences to be passive consumers. But communication is always a two-way process and this two-way 'acting-back' has been recognized by some archaeologists as an essential and desirable part of the relationship between archaeology and its publics and something to be actively embraced as part of the practice of a public archaeology. Accordingly, current practice recognizes two different sets of principles to be applied in conducting outreach: how to 'educate' the public; and how to encourage archaeologists and the public to interact.

'Telling' the past

THE ARCHAEOLOGICAL SITE RECREATED IN THE MUSEUM: THE CASE OF BARQUISIMETO, VENEZUELA

In 1990 the Second World Archaeological Congress was held in Barquisimeto, the third commercial city of Venezuela and the most important agriculturally. To mark the event a number of special exhibitions were mounted in local museums and in Barquisimeto Museum itself this took the form of the recreation of a local archaeological site under excavation. The exhibit showed in particular the distinctive South American technique for excavating human remains – whereby skeletons are left on pillars of earth which show the underlying stratigraphy – and the tools used by archaeologists. It also recreated the archaeologist in the form of a life-size cardboard figure and the archaeologist's ancillary requirements – a tent for use as finds hut, another tent as living space, a gas

127

cooker and a washing line complete with drying underpants. Although by no means to be interpreted as a 'real' site, the exhibition created a strong enough illusion to give a particular idea of what the practice of field archaeology is like. The addition of small domestic details served to create a 'human interest' aspect to the overall message, which was how archaeology contributes to the understanding of the Venezuelan past. The past thus created formed the subject of the remainder of the museum's displays, which were limited entirely to the period prior to European conquest. To emphasize this temporal restriction, the displays culminated in a disturbing reconstruction of the grave of the area's first Conquistador governor: in a darkened space stands a large wooden cross with his armoured helmet on its top and his sword tied around the shaft.

ARCHAEOLOGY ON THE SITE ITSELF: THE CASE OF FLAG FEN, ENGLAND

A 'traditional' approach to showing the past through actual rather than pretend archaeological fieldwork has been put to excellent effect at Flag Fen, which is a Bronze Age site (c. 1000BC) on the outskirts of Peterborough discovered while cleaning the sides of a fenland drainage channel. The site itself is a wooden platform, originally surrounded by water and connected to dry land by a wooden causeway. Due to the wet conditions, organic preservation is particularly good and many fine and well-preserved artefacts have also been retrieved during the course of excavation. Originally interpreted as a habitation site with perhaps some defensive purpose, more recent work suggests that the site was in fact a ritual one connected to the deposition of objects in wet places (Pryor, 1991). Since 1989 the site has been open regularly to the public and – since funding by English Heritage (the national agency for archaeology in England; see Chapter 3) has been withdrawn in accordance with an agreement about the future of the site - entry fees are now the main source of revenue.

The Flag Fen public archaeology programme is based upon three explicit principles:

- the past must not be mystified;
- the past must not be cheapened or trivialized;

- every interpretation is capable of reinterpretation (Pryor, 1989: 61).

Tours comprise an introductory video, a museum display of artefacts, a guided tour to features of the site, including a Roman road which lies above the level of the wooden platform (thus introducing the ideas of stratigraphy and relative dating), the ongoing excavation itself and examples of modern conservation and Bronze Age woodworking techniques. The site is further enhanced by the presence of replica Bronze Age (small) and Iron Age (larger) 'round houses' and examples of the kinds of animals that might have been kept by the ancient inhabitants of the area. The original use of excavation team members to conduct tours has been overtaken in recent years by the employment of specialist guides.

Although the site is very overtly 'presented' to its public, rather than inviting the public to participate directly in its interpretation, there is scope for interaction between guides and visitors. From the outset, it was expected that local people and those with particular kinds of skill or knowledge – such as carpenters and woodworkers – would offer advice on interpreting the material presented on the tour (Pryor, 1989). The change in interpretation of the site from domestic to ritual is also made very clear to visitors, along with the reasons for the change. The flow of information is inevitably largely one-way, bearing in mind the age of the site which would have been invisible to visitors to the area two thousand years ago, since when the fenland landscape has undergone further significant changes, some of which resulted in the discovery of the site.

Involving others

There is increasingly a body of opinion in archaeology across the English-speaking world that if there is any point in engaging with our audience, then it lies in giving those on whose behalf we work the ability to make judgements about what we do, how we do it and upon the pasts that we produce. In my own work I call this 'giving eyes to see with' – that is, granting to others the knowledge and skill to see what the trained archaeologist can see and to experience what we experience. To some extent, it may be an exercise in making our public 'people like us', so that non-archaeologists may better appreciate the work done in their name and often with their money. There are, however, other reasons – sometimes concerning social and political motives and agendas and the place of archaeology in the present – for doing so (cf. Tilley, 1989a, who considers archaeological excavation in terms of performance).

THE MUSEUM AS WORKSPACE: THE CASE OF SCHOOL PARTIES AT ELY MUSEUM, ENGLAND

Museums are particular kinds of places where particular kinds of people come together to do particular kinds of things (see Chapter 3). One of the tasks of running an educational programme based in a museum is that of overcoming the common assumption that a museum is really a classroom located outside school premises and that museum archaeologists are really – or at least should be – teachers. A common assumption among educational visitors seems to be that the most appropriate behaviour for children in the muscum is to sit quietly and be talked 'at', rather than for them to be turned loose to explore the space of the museum for themselves. The most commonly provided aid is a 'worksheet' – a piece of paper with a series of fixed questions and activities on it. The traditional emphasis is, therefore, upon control within a controlled space, on keeping visitors quiet and on the purposeful and pre-ordered study of the objects in cases. The alternative is free movement around the space, interaction with others who work in the space and the excitement and discovery of the space itself.

Museums, libraries and monuments to the dead (Merriman, 1991: 62–3) are all considered to be places for quiet contemplation and measured behaviour and it is easy to see how the association between museums and these other institutions comes about if one is expected from an early age to regard museums as places for this kind of behaviour pattern. What is perhaps less easy to understand is why museum staff and teachers in the early twenty-first century should so happily subscribe to the same attitudes, especially in an age when the educational emphasis is upon discovery and the excitement of learning (cf. Planel, 1990: 272). The approach in Ely Museum was to greet school parties with a brief introduction which emphasized the nature of the museum as a particular kind of activity-space – and then to turn them loose to explore it for themselves. Thereafter, the role of the museum curator was to obtain keys to a particular cabinet for closer inspection of the objects inside or to fetch a similar object from the reserve collection, one that could be held and touched. Worksheets were found to be generally educationally valueless: the brighter pupils are easily bored once it is complete; the remainder are mostly merely kept busy by it but not engaged; the small group who find it difficult are increasingly stressed by having to complete what is – in effect – an unnecessary examination paper. The latter group are those who may never voluntarily enter a museum again.

The expectation that schoolchildren should behave in a controlled way in a museum has much to do with the association between learning and the classroom. Museums are 'educational' places but they are not, in general, peopled by educators in the narrow sense. Where we employ professional educators to work with schools, the museum is often turned into a classroom space and may have spaces in it turned into classroom-type rooms, with blackboards and school seating and all the paraphernalia of formal teaching. But that is not what we do in museums. In museums we care for, preserve, interpret and make available to the public objects of historic and other interest. There is great scope for introducing that *work* to an audience by the people who actually do it.

THE ARCHAEOLOGICAL SITE AS PRODUCTION AREA: THE CASE OF VICAR'S FARM, CAMBRIDGE, ENGLAND

Similar considerations apply to the archaeological excavation site. Rather than focusing on formal talks and the specifics of what the site can tell about a particular period in the past, it is possible to de-emphasize the specifics of finds, maximize interaction between visitors and site staff and focus intensely on the practices of archaeology.

This approach requires first a short introductory talk outlining what visitors should keep an eye out for: how to identify features by changes in soil colour, for instance, and what site staff are actually doing, which might include drawing a plan or section, filling in a context sheet or talking to a colleague about how to proceed, as well as actually digging. It is followed by a tour of the site, led by a member of the site team rather than by one of those brought in to help with site visits. Along the way, other members of the team should be encouraged to pop up out of trenches to explain what they are doing. At the end, the processes of post-excavation analysis can be introduced by using the example of finds processing, from washing through identification to museum-style display. Overall, the emphasis here will be upon the practices of archaeologists and the experience of being on site during the process of excavation. The response of schools and excavators to this style of presentation is mutually reinforcing. Both have testified to having had a valuable and rich *experience* – something that could not be gained without direct interaction between site staff and visitors.

THE TOWNSCAPE AS ONGOING HISTORY: THE CASE OF THE BATTLEFIELD OF ST ALBANS, ENGLAND

The purpose of the Bloody Meadows Project (Carman, 1999a; 1999b) is to investigate historic battlefields of all periods from a broadly 'phenomenological' perspective (cf. Tilley, 1994). The aim is not so much to attempt to recreate what the battlefield was like on the day of battle but rather to explore the historicity of particular kinds of places through the experience of the physical remains of their pasts.

In terms of a 'public' archaeology, this approach means walking an audience through the space with a keen eye to the different periods of history and different human uses of the space, represented by buildings, monuments, street plans, different kinds of land-use and different shapes of ground. The result is a kind of 'time travel' – not a one-way trip into a singular and particular past and back, but a real journey through various times, where different pasts and an immediate present are met in juxtaposition. Places have histories that are evident in the experiences of them and it is in experiencing them as places that the histories become evident. The place has meaning because it has a history and that history is manifested in the material evidences of its past which testify to interesting and different pasts. These material things create the drama of the place which is the experience of its history in the present. It is this historicity that such a 'phenomenological' approach to historic battlefields can produce. In taking such an approach, and in being deliberately aware of both past and present in a particular place, the line that lies between the past and the present is walked, where neither dominates the other. Instead, they interact in interesting and challenging ways. It is not a search for an experience of being in the past, but rather an experience in the present which simultaneously reflects and derives from the contribution of history to a particular place. In the case of a historic battlefield, it is not an experience of ancient slaughter, but an experience of a particular place in the present as read through its history as manifested in material form. This history inevitably includes the event of the battle that was fought there, but not exclusively. It is that experience of being in the place that is captured.

CRITICAL THEORY APPLIED: THE CASE OF HISTORICAL ARCHAEOLOGY IN ANNAPOLIS, USA

One of the inspirations for the three previous examples is the work of Mark Leone and Parker B. Potter at Annapolis in the USA (Leone, *et al.* 1987; Potter, 1994; Potter and Leone, 1986; 1987; 1992). Taking inspiration from the post-Marxist critical theory of the Frankfurt School and using a series of devices to focus visitor attention – a 20-minute audio-visual presentation, interpretive on-site signs, a guided tour of archaeological activity and a self-guided tour of the city led by a handbook – the aim is to reveal how 'many aspects of contemporary ... life [in a capitalist economy] that are taken for granted are neither natural nor inevitable' (Potter, 1997: 36). 'Archaeology in Annapolis' was accordingly and expressly an attempt to create 'a critical archaeology [that could] inspire enlightenment [and] lead to emancipatory social action' (Potter, 1997: 36). The tours themselves were always led by active members of the site teams rather than by specialist presenters, although advised by a performance artist (Potter, 1997: 40–3). They focused on two areas: the archaeological evidence for the roots of modern everyday life and, especially, the current dominant ideology in a capitalist economy; and how versions of the past that serve the narrow interests of dominant social groups can be passed off – indeed accepted by subordinate groups - as 'objective' and 'universal'.

Such an approach focuses very much on the role of history in identity formation. In Annapolis, that identity has traditionally been forged by a number of elements: the presence of the US Naval Academy; the city's place as the State capital; as a port of call for pleasure boaters; as a tourist town; as an expressly 'historical' place; and as a 'small' town (bearing in mind that the USA generally sees itself as a nation made up not of its major cities but of lots of small communities) (Potter, 1994: 46–56). Current economic and social dynamics of the Annapolis community can be seen to revolve around the relationships between the town, the State of which it is the capital and the (Federal) Naval Academy, together with issues of gentrification, the rise of public housing and issues of tourism and development (Potter, 1994: 57–68). In turn, these themes are reflected in aspects of Annapolis' 'standard' history: a vision of the gentility of its population and a consequently ambiguous urban identity and the siting of the city by the water which encourages a measure of transience among its people (Potter, 1994: 82–8). These in turn lead to a general acceptance of certain 'inherent' historical qualities to which Annapolis and its people can lay claim, an emphasis on an imagined colonial 'Golden Age' and the fragmentation of various fields of study so that historical elements which do not fit this vision can be conveniently excluded (Potter, 1994: 104–15). In Annapolis, for Potter (1994: 117–21), the past is most generally used as a diversion from problems of the present, as a means of establishing precedents for current policies and as a means of establishing and maintaining degrees of social precedence among people. Accordingly, by emphasizing the imperative of preserving the remains of the past – to serve the tourist industry, to keep the 'character' of the city and as a reminder to its people of who 'they' are - the means by which the identity of Annapolis can be created and maintained becomes that very preservation of a particular kind of past (Potter, 1994: 123–31).

'Archaeology in Annapolis' (as the project was named) aimed to overcome the particular dominant ideology by revealing the alternative stories buried in its archaeology and especially the mechanisms by which the dominant ideology establishes itself (cf. Leone, 1984). It also sought to reveal the different voices that the dominant ideology kept silent – 'women, children, foot soldiers and sailors, slaves, freed slaves, Native Americans ..., the insane, the gaoled, as well as anybody else who has ever used a dish, a chamber-pot, room, privy, or medicine-bottle' (Leone *et al.*, 1995: 110). In particular, an attempt to broaden the scope to reveal the voices of the hitherto-silent Black population of Annapolis led to a joint project resulting in a museum display of artefacts from excavations at sites occupied by African-Americans as informed by oral testimony (Leone *et al.*, 1995). This responded to various pleas from consultees: to establish that African-Americans had archae-ology; to talk not of slavery but of freedom; and to inform as to the continuance of African traditions among the Black population of the city (Leone *et al.*, 1995: 112). The results – albeit tentative – suggested that although there exists a rich legacy of African-American archaeology, the use of material culture did not differ significantly between Black people and Whites; that a large free African-American population had inhabited Annapolis throughout the nineteenth and early twentieth centuries; and that very little of a distinctively 'African' tradition was evident.

The Annapolis experiment is a useful model for a publicly engaged archaeology, but despite intentions it never quite ceased to be a one-way process. Potter's language is instructive: 'In Annapolis, what we *teach* is ...' (Potter, 1997: 36, emphasis added). However, it is also clear that it was a process of opening up dialogue about issues in the present, such as tourism (Potter and Chabot, 1997: 46–8) and the place of the past in the present generally:

> Instead of seeing an archaeological site as some kind of 'cache' of truths about the past just waiting to be liberated from the ground, we prefer to see on-site archaeological interpretation as an important way of using sites as an environment in which a relatively wide range of truths about the past may be identified, developed, discussed and negotiated. Initiating dialogues can ... be a far less tidy undertaking than simply providing the facts about a particular piece of the past – but ... we are willing to give up having the final word in exchange for the benefits of being able to hear all kinds of interesting voices other than our own. (Potter and Chabot, 1997: 53)

'ARCHAEOLOGY FROM BELOW': THE CASE OF SEDGEFORD, ENGLAND

The shift towards an even more democratic approach in archae-ology is also evident in certain circles in the UK. At Sedgeford,

Norfolk, Neil Faulkner advocates such a democratic approach as a reaction against what he sees as the increasingly 'bureaucratic-professional tendency' in British archaeology (Faulkner, 2000: 22–5), which is similar to some of the processes outlined in Chapters 3 and 4. He accuses 'rescue' archaeology, which derives from development control policies, of applying the same standards to all projects, regardless of their diversity. He also points out that a presumption in favour of preservation (a principle underlying much public archaeology in a bureaucratic sense: Chapters 2 and 3) means that much of the archaeological resource remains largely unknown (Faulkner, 2000: 26–7). At the same time, rescue excavation is carried out for the purpose of retrieving what information is available in a short time, not because the site has been chosen to answer certain research questions but merely because it is in danger of destruction, and the result is often the application of standardized recording systems. However, he argues, in good archaeology the material encountered, the methods employed and the interpretations produced all interact and, indeed, are dependent upon one another. Faulkner's argument is, therefore, that while 'rescue' archaeology – concerned exclusively with the production of 'facts' divorced from interpretation and indeed understanding – is positivist and empiricist in approach, 'research' archaeology is much more dialectical in its process (Faulkner, 2000: 26–8).

As an alternative to an undemocratic, 'top-down' archaeology he promotes 'archaeology from below' which involves communities in the archaeology of their area. The principles represented by the Sedgeford project assert that sites should not be 'preserved' but should be investigated for what they can tell us about the past – the entire past, not just certain periods – of the locality. Using local volunteers, voluntary involvement by professionals, relying on contributions in kind to finance the project and by adopting a non-hierarchical structure to encourage initiative among the team, the project seeks to present an alternative to archaeology by professional contracting units supported by state bureaucracies. It also asserts the message that 'there is no single correct method in research', but that the greater the experience of an archaeologist in encountering the archaeological record, 'the more likely it is that critical engagement in the complex relationship between material, method and meaning will produce new ideas' (Faulkner, 2000: 32). In challenging the more bureaucratic 'rescue' style of archaeological heritage management, this style of 'public archaeology' in the narrow sense seeks to reassert the connection between archaeology as a public endeavour and archaeology as a research process (a relationship generally sundered: see Chapter 1).

The archaeologist as servant

So far in this chapter, the idea of a 'we' who are archaeologists and 'others' who are not 'us' has been treated as fairly straightforward. Such a treatment carries with it the idea that what is 'ours' does not belong to others and therefore allows – among other things – archaeologists to treat others as people to be taught about those things in which we are experts. It also allows archaeologists – as experts in the study of ancient things – to appropriate materials that fall within the realm of archaeological study, effectively taking them away from the communities whose heritage they represent. Over the course of the past twenty years, such behaviour has become increasingly the focus of challenge – from outside archaeology as well as from within. The result has been the development of a different style of treating the communities whose heritage engages archaeological attention.

The reburial issue

The 'trigger' for changed relations between archaeologists and others was one particular issue with global instances and repercussions. Often the discussion of these changed relations is subsumed under the title of 'the reburial issue' (cf. *World Archaeological Bulletin* 6, 1992; Skeates, 2000: 22–30), and is usually limited to the issue as it has played out in the USA, but it is in reality a broader concern. Jane Hubert (1989) conveniently summed up the global arguments around the reburial of human remains held by archaeologists, pointing out the variety of attitudes that exist in terms of the treatment of the dead. Archaeologists claim the supremacy of science for the retrieval and study of human remains. Others, however, such as Native Americans, Australian Aboriginal people and certain religious groups, find the removal of the dead from their resting place grossly offensive, both to the dead and to the living. In the case of minority indigenous peoples, archaeologists can be seen to represent a parasitic dominant White culture which treats the indigenous populations as inferior beings and works by denying indigenous people access to their traditional ways of life and cultural places. In taking the dead away for study, they break the ancient link that exists between a people and the land on which they live. Restoration of the dead to a place of rest serves to give back the dignity that was denied by the initial removal and also opens the way for claims to be made for land and the official recognition of ways of life.

The intransigence of some archaeologists in response to calls for the return of human remains to the communities from whom they had been taken led at least one palaeoanthropologist to change his position on the issue. Instead he adopted an oppositional stance to the increasingly narrow sense in which the field of archaeology was becoming professionalized, which he castigated as 'racist' in effect if not intent (Zimmerman, 1989b). Elsewhere, he outlined the differences in worldview represented by Native American and archaeological attitudes to the dead (Zimmerman, 1989a). Different conceptions of time promoted different understandings of the place of the dead in the world and different ideas about the appropriateness of applying laws affirmed or denied property rights in human remains. Overarching this, different understandings about each other's purpose in making a claim on the remains of the dead intensified conflict rather than serving to promote common interest in the remains of the past.

In response to these problems, the 1990 Federal US *Native American Graves Protection and Repatriation Act* (NAGPRA) effectively requires consultation between Federal archaeologists and museum personnel with representatives of the indigenous population on the future of human remains in the hands of archaeologists and in museum collections. While not all archaeologists are happy at the development nor all Native Americans satisfied and some persisting problems remain to be solved while other new ones emerge, it marks a major shift in the power relations between European–American scholars and others. NAGPRA has led to the passage of laws at the State level in the USA to cover non-Federal public archaeology and sometimes to extend coverage to the dead of European–American and other local communities. In addition, organizations such as the US-based SAA, AAA and ROPA (mentioned in Chapter 3) have included a specific concern for the dead of other cultures in their Codes of Practice and similar provisions are included in the Code of Ethics of the Australian Archaeological Association (Davidson *et al.*, 1995: 83).

Beyond the dead: descendant communities

Out of the issues surrounding the reburial issue have emerged new ways of working with the people whose pasts are investigated and interpreted by archaeologists. In 1991, the Australian Archaeological Association sought to establish a new code of ethics for archaeologists working with indigenous people and to do so organized a conference where some examples of work considered 'good' could be presented. These projects fell into three main types: research involving Aboriginal communities; research requested by Aboriginal communities; and co-operative work deriving from the imperatives of CRM (Davidson *et al.*, 1995). In all cases the role of the indigenous people themselves is emphasized: as consultees whose permission was required before work could go ahead, as clients determining what work would be conducted and as partners in joint projects. Similar concerns led to a series of sessions at meetings of the American Archaeological Association in which new relationships with Native American peoples were addressed. Adopting the language of processual archaeology, this was seen as a process of altering the 'paradigm' (the way of thinking) dominant among American archaeologists studying the pre-Columbian past. In turn this included integrating the scientific approach to the past represented by American archaeology with more traditional understandings (cf. Zimmerman, 1989a) establishing the usefulness and relevance of archaeology to Native Americans and the manner and consequences of consultation, especially following NAGPRA (Swidler *et al.*, 1997).

Meanwhile, individuals have been working to establish truly co-operative working practices with the descendants of those whose past is under study. In the USA, archaeologists have collaborated with Native Americans to reinterpret events in nineteenth-century American history which will serve to reinsert their experience back into an understanding of the American past. In particular, both in the case of the Cheyenne outbreak from Fort Robinson in 1879 (McDonald *et al.*, 1991) and the Battle of the Little Bighorn (Scott *et al.*, 1989), Native accounts of these events – previously dismissed and overborne by US military accounts – have been vindicated by archaeological research. To some extent, working with – rather than dictating to - the communities whose past is under study is a question of 'good manners' rather than anything else (Field *et al.*, 2000: 42, citing Pardoe, 1992: 140). Issues identified in the work of Judith Field and her Aboriginal colleagues included the attitude of the archaeologist and the need to establish a relationship based upon trust. In turn, these included active participation by the community in the project (cf. Faulkner, 2000), handling human remains with respect and regard for tradition and the concerns of the living, maintaining continuity of personnel and contact and sharing information and ensuring access both to information and material (Field *et al.*, 2000: 42–5). However, such concerns are not only the province of dealing with indigenous populations, but of dealing with any people whose past is under scrutiny (cf. McDavid and Babson, 1997). The Jordan Plantation site in Brazoria, Texas, is one where descendants of both former enslaved people and former slave-owners are working together, combining archaeology with family and genealogical histories. Here the archaeologists are very much the servants of the local people and are developing a number of techniques to encourage a democratic 'conversation' about the past and present relationships, including the use of a website (www.webarchaeology.com) to encourage participation (McDavid, 1999). The project draws heavily upon the American tradition of 'pragmatist' philosophy for inspiration (McDavid, 2000) and the focus is always upon the process of engaging with others about their past (McDavid, 1997; forthcoming). It is in work such as this that perhaps any message for the future lies.

Conclusion

There has been a common perception shared by museum professionals, archaeologists and teachers that the proper atmosphere for learning is one of being taught. This may explain why there is a great temptation among archaeologists engaged in public outreach to try to be educators in the narrow sense and to turn the places where we work into classrooms, rather than allowing them to be the kinds of places they actually are. And yet that is the great strength of such places: that they are not classrooms but *real* places in their own right which have their own characteristics and attributes. Some of these characteristics and attributes derive from the fact that they represent the heritage of living people, and it is therefore important that we recognize that they are not ours to do with as we wish.

It is in exploring and experiencing the characteristics and attributes of places and things that a public archaeology can offer more than mere teaching. Museums, working excavations and historic places are very different kinds of things from one another; very different too from modern schools, homes and workplaces. They may represent different traditions and ways of life in the present as well as in the past. It is by being different that they can enrich us and others and it is that experience which can be offered not only by us to others but by others to us. This is in a sense a 'real' public archaeology: not 'outreach' but sharing; not an archaeological monologue about the past, but a dialogue about ourselves with other people. If one of the purposes of a public archaeology is to justify archaeology, then there must be more to public archaeology than merely telling people the stories about the past we wish to pass on. It must also involve showing people what we do, giving them the experience of what we do and allowing them to share themselves with us even if this means they drive the archaeological process. In the places where we work – in museums, on site, in laboratories, in landscapes – we have the resources to let us do that. The more important resource remains always ourselves and the experience of what we do.

Further reading

Principles of presentation

Belcher, M. (1991) *Exhibitions in Museums*. Leicester: Leicester University Press.

English Heritage (1988) *Visitors Welcome! A Manual on the Presentation and Interpretation of Archaeological Remains*. London: English Heritage.

Uzzell, D. (ed.) (1989a) *Heritage Interpretation: Volume 1. The Natural and Built Environment*. London: Belhaven Press.

Presenting the past

Ballantyne, R. and Uzzell, D. (eds) (1998) *Contemporary Issues in Heritage and Environmental Interpretation*. London: The Stationery Office.

Jameson, J. H. (1997) *Presenting Archaeology to the Public: Digging for Truths*. Walnut Creek, CA: Altamira Press.

Potter, P. B. (1994) *Public Archaeology in Annapolis: A Critical Approach to History in Maryland's Ancient City*. Washington, DC: Smithsonian Institution Press.

Stone, P. and MacKenzie, R. (eds) (1990) *The Excluded Past: Archaeology in Education*. London: Routledge.

Stone, P. and Molyneaux B. L. (eds) (1994) *The Presented Past: Heritage, Museums and Education*. London: Routledge.

Uzzell, D. (ed.) (1989b) *Heritage Interpretation: Volume 2. The Visitor Experience*. London: Belhaven Press.

Relations with descendant communities

Carmichael, D. L., Hubert, J., Reeves, B. and Schanche, A. (eds) (1994) *Sacred Sites, Sacred Places*. London: Routledge.

Davidson, I., Lovell-Jones, C. and Bancroft, R. (1995) *Archaeologists and Aborigines Working Together*. Armidale, NSW: University of New England Press.

Layton, R. (ed.) (1989a) *Conflict in the Archaeology of Living Traditions*. London: Routledge.

Layton, R. (ed.) (1989b) *Who Needs the Past? Indigenous Values and Archaeology*. London: Routledge.

McDavid, C. and Babson, D. (eds) (1997) *In the Realm of Politics: Prospects for Public Participation in African–American Archaeology.* California: Society for Historical Archaeology (= *Historical Archaeology* 31.3).

Swidler, N., Dongoske, K. E., Anyon, R. and Downer, A. S. (1997) *Native Americans and Archaeologists: Stepping Stones to Common Ground.* Walnut Creek, CA: Altamira Press.

World Archaeological Bulletin 6 (1992) Special issue on the Reburial Issue.

Summary points

1. The discourse of 'public archaeology' – in the sense of communication with those outside the discipline of archaeology – is generally in terms of specific case studies of individual encounters. This means that there is no established generalized discourse, one that takes a historical or global perspective on developments over time. It also encourages a style of discussion based upon the promotion of certain particular styles, rather than a concern for understanding the effects and consequences of approaches.

2. Styles and forms of display and exhibition reflect the purposes and the philosophy of the institution from which they come. They also inevitably reflect the historical conditions of their making, and these can change, so there is never a complete permanence.

3. A one-way style of presentation – 'teaching' or 'telling' the past – disengages the archaeologist from the audience and encourages a passive receptivity. Other approaches are possible which result in a two-way flow of information and ideas.

4. The 'reburial issue' – concerning the return to indigenous communities of human remains for treatment in accordance with the community's traditions – has brought about a change in the relations between archaeologists and the communities whose past they study. Widespread consultation with indigenous communities is increasingly the norm, supported by Codes of Professional Ethics and occasionally by law.

5. Other archaeologists go beyond consultation to act as servants of

the communities whose past they study, sometimes at the request of the community. In promoting a full partnership between archaeology and descendant communities, this can go towards the creation of a 'true' public archaeology, one at the service of communities rather than parasitic upon them.

Objects on show

Plate 5.1 Archaeology on show in Barquisimeto Museum, Venezuela ...

Plate 5.2 ... and the real thing: skeletons left atop columns of earth, Venezuela

Plate 5.3 Traditional Venezuelan crafts 1: pots in a reconstructed context. Barquisimeto Museum, Venezuela

Plate 5.4 Traditional Venezuelan crafts 2: textiles in a reconstructed context. Barquisimeto Museum, Venezuela

Plate 5.5 Roman walls, London, England: incorporated into both the Museum of London and the Barbican Centre

6 The Value 'Debate' in Archaeology

Concepts of value underpin much of the discourse of heritage as set out in previous chapters since they relate directly to ideas about the purpose of creating a category of 'heritage' set apart from other categories of things. However, much of the effort to discuss questions of value in the heritage literature has been concerned to reduce them to issues of practicality. As a result, so many of the discussions in print can appear to be merely about technical issues of practice, rather than philosophical in approach and therefore concerned with generating greater understanding. Despite this, deep philosophical differences inform the discussion of issues of value which it is worthwhile bringing to the fore. Accordingly, this chapter will emphasize the similarity of structure of each of the three strands of overt discussion about the value of material remains which are covered within it. They can each claim to represent at least one of the major principles that drive archaeological heritage management practice globally. While the literature of archaeology generally fails to acknowledge it - and frequently pretends that is not true – each set of ideas about value in archaeology nevertheless derives from ideas which have their origin in disciplines outside, and even alien to, archaeology. Drawing further on this point of origin, each presents a relevant scheme of value – a manner of measuring value - deemed to be appropriate and from this emerge various specific types of value to be applied to archaeological material.

These similarities in the structure of approaches to value, however, are overborne by differences of content. Accordingly, although each has the capacity to influence - and be influenced by - others, in practice they are discussed quite separately and thus represent a series of 'closed' discourses. Of these three different approaches, one has been applied so far only to the museum sector although it has the capacity to spread beyond the museum to the heritage more generally, including archaeology, and discussion has largely been phrased as a technical matter of accounting technique. Another has become the dominant approach in archaeology, where discussion has been limited almost entirely to the literature of archaeology. The third does not represent a practical approach but is a deliberate attempt to approach issues of value from a more philosophical direction. All of these concern the valuation of types of material (see Chapter 2) but contained within them is the possibility of movement away from – or beyond – this: the final section of the chapter therefore addresses the option of valuing archaeological practice rather than the material which is its object.

The accountability of institutions

It is an axiom of archaeological heritage management that the remains of the past are 'public' (as discussed in Chapters 1 and 4). From this principle – that 'there is no such thing as "private archaeology" (McGimsey, 1972: 5) – derives the idea that the heritage is and should be held in and by public institutions, such as museums and State agencies, for and on behalf of the wider community. These institutions are funded out of the public purse and act in the public name and for 'the public good' (Chapter 3) and from this 'public' purpose it further derives that they should be directly accountable to the public on whose behalf they carry out their work. In order to be publicly accountable, it becomes necessary for these institutions to provide regular reports on their activities and the costs of doing so and this is common practice across the world. Sometimes the reports produced are fully publicly available and sometimes are made to other public bodies, such as government departments or legislatures. Out of this train of conventional logic has risen the practice applied to non-profit-making public museums in Australia that they should include in their reports a monetary value for their collections, for the purposes of financial reporting (Carnegie and Wolnizer 1995; Carman *et al.*, 1999).

Museums and collections as economic entities

In treating museums from an expressly economic perspective, Johnson and Thomas (1991: 5) emphasize that one of their central concerns as economists 'is the efficiency with which resources ... are allocated to different uses'. In attempting to achieve this, they are concerned with a number of factors which interact. Among them are: understanding the nature and scale of the museum sector of the economy (the British economy in this case); the outputs from museum activities for which demand may exist; the structure of the demand for those museum services; the costs of providing those services; and how these relate to issues such as public funding and entry pricing policy.

The direct product of a museum – its 'output' – is essentially scholarly, in the form of the fruits of research into the contents of its collections, which then lead to more tangible outputs such as 'publications, lectures and the development of exhibitions' (Johnson and Thomas, 1991: 17). These in turn lead to further – more intangible – outputs in the form of the 'experience' enjoyed by visitors, which is not merely dependent upon the content and form of exhibitions (issues mentioned in Chapter 5), but also such necessary other elements as the provision of:

> toilet facilities, catering and retailing. ... [Beyond the museum itself, the experience may also include] anticipation and subsequent memories of a visit ... [and] videos and publications[. In addition] the *number* of visitors will often be an important influence on the average visitor experience. (Johnson and Thomas, 1991: 18–9, emphasis in original)

G La Sto.

Additional 'spillover' effects can also accrue so that 'one individual's "consumption" of a publication may have an educative effect on others [and] someone who has made a visit ... may generate greater knowledge and appreciation of the past in others' (Johnson and Thomas, 1991: 19). In endeavouring to establish an appropriate level of public funding for museums, it becomes necessary to take into account these outputs, the existing demand for them and the costs of their provision. Since economic demand consists in a measure of how much an individual will pay for a particular product (Johnson and Thomas, 1991: 26–8) a conventional economic argument would suggest that where sufficient demand exists for a particular output, this could be charged to individual visitors or purchasers. This could serve to reduce or even eradicate the need for public funding. Such an approach, however, does not take sufficient account of other kinds of demand which do not attach to individuals. These include the 'spillover' effects (cited above) which accrue from visitors and others who take advantage of the museum's outputs, the desire among some people to have the museum available for use in the future, the desire among sections of the community that others should have the opportunity to use the museum even if they choose not to do so (cf. Merriman, 1991), and the demand for museum services that may exist among future generations (Johnson and Thomas, 1991: 28–9).

Efficiency, output and valuation

All of these kinds of demand relate directly to the nature of the museum as a public institution and may require a measure of public support. In deciding the level of such support, an accurate understanding of costs is vital, for as Johnson and Thomas explain:

> Any examination of the allocation of resources requires an accurate picture of the costs that arise from utilizing those resources. The key concept of the economist is opportunity cost: the cost of using a resource is the best return it could obtain in some alternative use. (Johnson and Thomas, 1991: 23)

However, they go on to point out that the costs of a museum providing services can be relatively fixed or otherwise constrained: accordingly, the option of demonstrating improving efficiency by the reduction of costs may not be available. The alternative is to show how good is the performance of museum functions, which can include a range of different measures for different functions, including the 'attraction' represented by the museum taking all its attributes into account (Martin, 1994), visitor accessibility, financial effectiveness, staffing, collection use and collection growth (Ames, 1994: 25–30). The latter is measured by Ames (1994: 30) in terms of the number of new accessions or items conserved relative to the number of items in the collection overall, but in Australia public museums are required to go further and measure the value of the collection in financial terms. Much of the subsequent debate concerning the propriety of labelling museum collections as financial assets has revolved around technical issues of definition and accounting practice; although it is an issue with international repercussions, it has been largely limited to Australia (Carnegie and Wolnizer, 1995; 1996; 1999; Hone, 1997; Micallef and Peirson, 1997). The potential importance of the issue is, however, reflected in two aspects: the trend across the world towards the application of accounting systems into all areas of public life (Power 1996); and its potential for extension to all other types of heritage object (as advocated by Micallef and Peirson, 1997: 32).

As a body of materials held for particular purposes (Chapter 2), museum collections directly contribute to the ability of a museum to fulfil its functions (Chapter 3). These functions are for the public good and can be understood from an economic perspective, as Johnson and Thomas (1991) have shown. From the perspective of accounting, therefore, collections can be argued to represent a source of 'future economic benefits controlled by' the museum and this definition makes them 'assets' as understood in accounting discourse (Micallef and Peirson, 1997: 31). On this basis, it is argued, they should be shown in the museum's financial accounts as assets with an appropriate monetary value placed upon them. Since financial quantities can be held to be unambiguous measures of value (but see McSweeney, 1997), the justification for this is that over time it would allow an assessment of 'whether the value ... has been eroded, improved, or retained [and thereby provide] some of the information necessary to enable assessments of [museum managers'] performance' (Micallef and Peirson, 1997: 34). In particular, it is claimed:

> a large part of the collections ... is in storage rather than on public display. Informed decisions about ... whether the level of items in storage is excessive ... cannot be made without information as to both the quantity and financial value of those items. Without information about the financial value of items in storage, there can be no informed assessment of the opportunity cost of holding these items. (Micallef and Peirson, 1997: 34)

The fallacy in such an argument about opportunity cost is that there are in practice – and frequently in law – no alternative 'opportunities' for the use of a museum collection, a monument, a heritage site or a work of art (Stanton and Stanton, 1998: 199), especially since the purpose of a museum collection is to be held by a museum for museum purposes (Chapters 2 and 3) rather than to be disposed of in the market. The problem of allocating a market value is compounded by the fact that many items held as 'heritage' objects – especially those deriving from archaeological activity, such as pottery sherds, soil samples and fragments of objects – will not attract a market price, however low. There are, however, alternative methods that can be applied. 'Replacement cost' or 'deprival value' is based upon the current cost of seeking to replace items in a collection should they be lost or destroyed: accordingly, items forming the archive of an excavation would be valued at the total cost of mounting an excavation of the same scale from which they first derived, together with any additional costs relating to post-excavation analysis, interpretation, conservation and placement in the museum. 'Contingent valuation' is based upon the statements of respondents as to the amount of money – whether as taxes or entrance fees – they are prepared to pay to maintain the existence of the museum or other heritage institution. Both may provide measurable financial values but may also lead to absurdities: 'replacement cost' may result in either very high or very low values being placed upon items in defiance of experience or common sense; 'contingent valuation' can take no account of those who believe that heritage institutions should be free. To the philosophical objection that heritage objects are not available for economic assessment, therefore, is added the practical difficulty of assessing financial value meaningfully.

Enabling accountability

Objections to the placing of a financial value upon collections and other kinds of heritage object do not challenge the preceding idea that heritage institutions themselves are economic entities (cf. Johnson and Thomas, 1991; Ames, 1994; Martin, 1994; Stanton and Stanton, 1998). Accordingly, the question of making decisions concerning resource allocation still stands and the issue of the public accountability of public institutions remains in place. Attention, however, shifts back to the institution itself and the 'social value' it provides. In particular, it becomes appropriate 'to focus future efforts on the nature of the organizational mission in non-profit museums ... [since] missions ... motivate staff and often substitute for profit as a criterion for success' (Rentschler and Potter, 1996: 110). A survey of the mission statements of a number of major Australian museums conducted in advance of such advice opened the way to a considered programme of accountability measures for public museums.

'Enabling Accountability in Museums' (EAM) (Carnegie and Wolnizer, 1996) draws upon ideas developed within the accounting field to establish a more sophisticated 'broad scope accountability' (Parker, 1996: 9) for public institutions than can be achieved by financial measures alone. In particular it focuses upon ways of measuring the 'vitality' and 'viability' of such organizations (Landry, 1994: 14). Viability refers to the long-term continuance of the organization and its ability to meet change and new circumstances. Vitality concerns the level of activity within the organization, the use made of its outputs, the relations between people and between people and activities within the institution and how the institution both projects itself and is perceived beyond its own walls. Viability is therefore a condition of the institution at any one time, while its level of vitality serves to determine its viability. Not all of the things a museum does can be measured meaningfully in quantitative or financial terms but this does not prevent them from being reported upon. Accordingly, rather than provide a financial valuation for the collection, EAM recommends the provision of information concerning the 'conduct of physical inventories [of the collection on a regular basis] and the correlation of inventory records and physical count data' (Carnegie and Wolnizer, 1996: 367–77). Similarly, the record of achievement of non-financial organizational goals can be reported upon (Carnegie and Wolnizer, 1996: 378) as can the use put to appropriate technologies (Carnegie and Wolnizer, 1996: 379–80).

Like Ames (1994, 25–30), EAM recommends the use of quantitative performance indicators of various kinds where possible, noting especially any variance between targeted performance levels and those actually achieved (Carnegie and Wolnizer, 1996: 377). But EAM does not abandon financial measures where these are appropriate, such as budget planning and management (Carnegie and Wolnizer, 1996: 377). It suggests the application of 'Activity-Based Management' analysis to certain types of activity, which identifies those activities within the normal work of the institution that add some kind of value to the collection or to the *Perf. Indius.* outputs of the institution and also those that do not; a knowledge of this can aid in future resource allocation (Carnegie and Wolnizer, 1996: 378). In terms of financial reports, it recommends three in particular: an operating statement, showing how incoming money was spent within the institution; a statement of external transactions, showing sources of income and the movement of money between the institution and its banks, debtors and creditors; and a statement of solvency, showing how debts owed by the institution have been financed. These financial statements, in turn, are designed to fulfil accountability criteria to be met by publicly owned institutions comprising: stewardship, cost of service, financial viability and responsibility reports (Carnegie and Wolnizer, 1996, 378–9). All of these represent the aims underpinning the development of EAM as an alternative to purely financial measures deriving from a narrow reading of accounting practice.

A 'useful' archaeology: significance and importance of sites

The premier axiom of archaeological heritage management is that the remains of the past are 'finite' and 'non-renewable' (Chapter 1; Darvill, 1987: 1; McGimsey, 1972: 24; Cleere, 1984c: 127). It follows from this that – since it is not possible to preserve everything from the past – they are subject to assessment for their archaeological 'significance' (Cleere, 1984c: 127; Dunnell, 1984; Shaafsma, 1989) and therefore their fitness for archaeological attention, whether as sites to be investigated or sites to be preserved. The practice of evaluating archaeological sites and remains has therefore become a central activity of heritage management globally (as discussed in Chapters 1 and 2) and at least one attempt has been made to extend its reach beyond archaeology proper to the museum (Young, 1994).

Questions of archaeological 'significance' or 'importance' are equally international (cf. Briuer and Mathers, 1996 for the USA; Sullivan and Bowdler, 1984 for Australia; Darvill *et al.* 1987, for the UK; Deeben *et al.*, 1999 for Europe; Wester, 1990 for West Africa). Having said this, however, the discourse of value represented by the international community is frequently different from that at the national level. Entry on the UNESCO World Heritage List (mentioned in Chapter 3) requires that items should be classed in terms of ascribed attributes, as 'a masterpiece', 'unique or exceptional' or 'outstanding', whereas national criteria are more likely to assess items in terms of 'inherent' qualities, more closely related to the specifics of the object (Table 6.1). In fact, the UK is one of the few countries with a prescribed set of criteria for the evaluation of its heritage places and also has one of the more sophisticated schemes for their application (Darvill *et al.*, 1987), although much of the discussion of 'significance' around the globe in practice concerns the agreement of such criteria.

Measuring archaeological significance

Briuer and Mathers (1996) have conveniently provided coverage of the development of the concept of 'archaeological significance' in the USA from 1974 to 1994, after which date much of the explicit discussion appears to wane (but for a revived interest in issues of value more generally, see Mathers *et al.*, forthcoming). The USA is the 'home' of the significance concept, which was enshrined in law and practice in the early 1970s. From there it has spread over to the rest of the globe (Smith, 1996; Wester, 1990).

In the literature reviewed by Briuer and Mathers (1996), several key issues were evident. The first, which received most attention in the literature, was a general agreement that the measurement of the archaeological value of a site is dynamic and relative; that is to say, it depends upon context and will vary over time (Briuer and Mathers, 1996: 11). One of the problems with the application of criteria for measuring the significance of sites, identified early on, was that they can only reflect current concerns and cannot foresee any that may emerge in the future. Such an idea is at the heart of one of the seminal papers concerning archaeological value in which Lipe (1984: 3) outlines how different values derive from particular

Table 6.1 Value criteria for inclusion on lists of heritage

Level	Criteria
Global – World Heritage List	It should: represent a masterpiece of human creative genius, or exhibit an important interchange of human values over a span of time or within a cultural area of the world, or developments in architecture, or technology, monumental arts, town planning or landscape design, or bear a unique or at least exceptional testimony to a cultural tradition or to a civilization which is living or has disappeared, or be an outstanding example of a type of building or architectural or technological ensemble, or land-scape which illustrates a significant stage or significant stages in human history, or be an outstanding example of a traditional human settlement or land-use which is representative of a culture or cultures, especially when it has become vulnerable under the impact of irreversible change, or be directly or tangibly associated with events or living traditions, with ideas or with beliefs, or with artistic and literary works of outstanding universal significance (a criterion used only in exceptional circumstances and together with other criteria). Equally important is the authenticity of the site and the way it is protected and managed.
National – UK National Importance (DoE, 1991)	Period Rarity and representativity Diversity of form Survival Group value Potential Documentation

contexts of use, how these in turn feed particular institutional structures and result in the preservation of particular kinds of remains. These preserved remains then form the 'cultural resource base' from which items will be selected in the next 'round'. In part, this consensus as to the dynamic and relative nature of the evaluation process must derive from a general feeling that 'significance' is the servant of archaeology rather than its determining master and should reflect specifically archaeological concerns. Accordingly, the second most discussed aspect of American CRM practice is the need for regional research designs, representing

> a continuing consensus ... for developing well-defined and intellectually rigorous regional frameworks for evaluating cultural resources, rather than restricting ... units of analysis to ... site-by-site phenomena or narrow and highly idiosyncratic criteria. The continued and widespread popularity of this concept is probably a function of its relationship and overlap with other frequently cited concepts ... that have become central to discussions of cultural significance. (Briuer and Mathers, 1996: 15)

These other concepts include the dynamic and relative nature of significance assessment, the accepted need for representative samples of sites, issues related to the establishment of archaeological preserves, the development of significance criteria and the question as to whether CRM work constitutes research archaeology or something different.

As an alternative to the problems inherent in selecting sites on the basis of their 'stand-alone' significance, much of the literature has advocated the preservation of representative samples of sites, to provide a stock on which different styles of research may be carried out: in the US, this has been designated 'conservation archaeology' (Lipe, 1974; Schiffer and Gumerman, 1977). In the UK, the idea of representative samples underlies the Monuments Protection Programme which is designed both to increase the number of sites protected under UK law and also to serve as a check on the quality of earlier decisions (Darvill *et al.*, 1987; Startin, 1993). In practice, a concern with 'significance-testing' and with representative samples both result in a call for clear criteria on which to make judgements, since neither significance nor representability can be assessed without standards against which to check them. A glance at several suggested sets of criteria (Table 6.2) indicates how similar such criteria tend to be across the world. While the list from Briuer and Mathers (1996: 14) is somewhat longer than those from the UK (Darvill *et al.*, 1987) and recommended for use across Europe (Deeben *et al.*, 1999) and is also somewhat less well structured – partly because it derives from diverse contributions to the literature rather than a single programme – it nevertheless becomes clear that they all recognize similar attributes of sites. In particular, all share a concern for periodicity and the historical periods when a site was in use, disguised by Deeben *et al.* (1999) as one part of rarity. Similarly, the amount of available information from other sources, the contribution the site may make to other fields of enquiry and the degree of survival of material or threats posed to the site are all taken into account in every scheme.

This similarity in measures of significance and representativity leads to one of the charges levelled at significance evaluation, whether carried out to establish site significance in the USA or Australia or 'national importance' in the UK: that it has nothing to do with archaeological research as such but is a bureaucratic practice (Carman, 2000: 10–18; Faulkner, 2000; cf. Renfrew, 1983). There are two counter-arguments to this. One is that the purpose of establishing protected sites, or archaeological preserves (Lipe, 1974), is to maintain a stock of undamaged sites for future investigations which will apply new techniques and different research agendas. The other is that the near-comprehensive review of US literature on significance from 1974 to 1994 indicates that 'with one notable exception . . . none of the publications . . . take the position that CRM is not research' (Briuer and Mathers, 1996: 17). That exception (Dunnell, 1984) equates research with inevitable destruction and CRM with a stark choice between preservation or destruction without recording, since the sites themselves are not sought on the basis of relevance to research but because they face destruction.

Table 6.2 Recommended assessment criteria for the significance/
importance and representativeness of sites

Country	Criteria		
USA (Briuer and Mathers, 1996: 14)	Chronological periods Quantity/diversity of material Dateable remains Presence of architectural features Archival records (documentation) Site type Site function Site size Physical integrity Cultural/ethnic affiliations Historic themes Environmental habitat Topographic setting Severity/immediacy of threat		
Europe (Deeben *et al.*, 1999)	Aesthetic value Historical value Integrity Preservation Rarity Research potential Group value Representivity		
UK (Darvill *et al.*, 1987)	*Characterization criteria* Period (currency) Rarity Diversity (form) Period (representativity)	*Discrimination criteria* Survival Group value (association) Potential Documentation Group value (clustering) Diversity (features) Amenity value	*Assessment criteria* Condition Fragility Vulnerability Conservation value

The 'useful' value of archaeology

As if to emphasize the difference between 'significance' as applied in US and Australian archaeology and 'importance' as measured in the UK, a particular strand of discussion has emerged in the British literature which seeks not just to describe the attributes and characteristics of sites suitable for evaluation but also to provide a philosophical and theoretical foundation for it. In seeking to identify 'value systems ... on the one hand connected to attitudinal arrangements and on the other to interest-based arrangements' Darvill (1995: 42) sought to understand the different and co-existing value systems applying to archaeology in the UK. Since, he argues, values result from a search for what is relevant and acceptable, knowledge is a crucial factor in determining the values people choose to hold. This places expert knowledge in particular at the centre of value formation as it relates to material which is the object of that expertise. Accordingly, in understanding the values placed upon archaeological remains, we must note that 'archae-ologists are both participants in the application of value systems through being members of society, and generators of more widely adopted values because they are experts in their field' (Darvill, 1995: 42). In other words, the values placed upon archaeological remains are archaeological values because they derive from the position of archaeologists as the arbiters of what is archaeological.

Darvill's (1995) analysis of the co-existing and competing values applied to archaeological remains presents a hierarchy under the two main heads of 'use values' and 'non-use values'; the latter comprises option and existence values (Table 6.3) in which each specific value derives from a particular attitude to the material being valued and a particular set of interests which that material may serve. The concepts of 'use' and 'non-use' values – the latter comprising 'option' and 'existence' values among others – derive from economics and, in particular, schemes designed to understand the 'social value' provided by non-profit-making institutions (cf. Johnson and Thomas, 1991; Martin, 1994).

For Darvill (1995: 43) use value 'is based upon consumption' of archaeological resources in the present, although this need not be destructive consumption. Its attitudinal orientation is grounded in

Table 6.3 Darvill's (1995) value systems for archaeology

Use values	Non-use values
Research	**Option values**
Creative arts	Social stability
Education	Mystery and enigma
Recreation and tourism	
Symbolic value	**Existence values**
Legitimization of	Cultural identity
current action	No change
Social solidarity	
Monetary gain	

'the standards and expectations of academic ... inquiry; and, increasingly, in the principle of resource allocation as upheld in modern societies which allows individuals and groups to gain from the fortuitous and uneven distribution of natural and humanly produced resources'. The interest-based orientation of use value depends upon the specific kind of use under consideration (Darvill, 1995: 44–5). Accordingly, as data, the archaeological resource is of benefit to archaeology and science more generally. It is also a source of inspiration to artists, writers and photographers as well as contributing to education more widely. Some individual sites and monuments attract many paying visitors each year, while others perform the role of landmarks for hikers and others to appreciate in their landscape setting. Archaeology – and the pasts it is able to represent – can have powerful symbolic meanings, which in turn allow its use for political purposes, to uphold a *status quo* or to promote a feeling of unity among a population. As tourist sites, as the source material from which commercial representations (books, films, souvenirs) can be derived and as items for sale in the market, archaeological heritage objects all have the capacity to generate monetary and economic gain.

For Darvill (1995: 46), option values represent a realm of 'production rather than consumption' directed not to the present 'but to some unspecified time in the future'. The attitudinal orientations of option value are 'grounded in altruistic principles and selfless behaviour where the future is better than the present'. Specific option values concern the maintenance of stability by avoiding change and preservation of elements of 'mystery and enigma' in relation to the past and its remains: accordingly, unlike the knowledge-based use values, 'new knowledge is rarely liberated and fed into the system' (Darvill, 1995: 46). Nevertheless 'option value carries with it a contradiction, because whilst as a value set it stands in opposition to use value, the realization of option value involves the redefinition of the values themselves' into a use value (Darvill, 1995: 47). Existence values relate 'simply to the existence of the resource ... [and] the interest-base is the psychological imperative in having a past, knowing of its well-being, without necessarily doing anything about it' (Darvill, 1995: 47). In particular, existence values relate to notions of cultural identity and resistance to change (Darvill, 1995: 47–8). For Darvill, 'conservatism, conservationism, and traditionalism are the steering principles' of option values (Darvill, 1995: 46) while existence values constitute simply 'a "feelgood" factor' (Darvill, 1995: 47).

It is interesting to compare Darvill's use of the ideas of these economically derived values with the uses made by economists themselves. For Darvill, use values emerge as positive, knowledge-driven and active; whereas non-use values are negative, resistant to new knowledge and passive. Accordingly they stand opposed to one another in a hierarchy of preference. However, the use made of the concepts of option and existence values by Johnson and Thomas (1991) and Martin (1994) is much more positive. For Johnson and Thomas (1991: 28–9), option values are treated as an integral and important part of the 'social value' of a museum, translating into 'option demand' for which individuals may be prepared to pay. This demand extends not only to others – because the 'holder' of the option may also wish others to have the option of visiting the museum - but also has a public good element since provision of the option for one does not exclude others from also enjoying that opportunity. Indeed, so long as the option is not acted upon (i.e. the museum is not visited by that individual at this moment) then the option has even greater public good value by providing space for another visitor. Existence value also forms part of 'merit good demand' as set out by Johnson and Thomas (1991: 29). For Martin

(1994: 257) both option and existence values form part of the matrix of 'motivations' which also include the willingness to bequest items or money to the institution, to pay taxes for its upkeep or to give gifts in the form of cash or kind.

In fact, both option and existence values are essentially deferred use values. The option value contains in it the idea of use at some point – by oneself or another – while the existence value is a form of option value indefinitely postponed. In practice they support one another and – rather than being mutually hostile – are merely different versions of one another where time is the only crucial factor. Therefore all Darvill's (1995) values are use values. The importance of his argument is not, however, undone by this criticism of it, for in making it he reveals an important aspect of all systems of archaeological valuation applied across the world: that they all derive from the economic concept of 'use value'. The kinds of criteria recommended or applied in assessing the significance or importance of sites all relate to various kinds of use, frequently scholarly use as the focus of research and understanding of the past but also, occasionally, as amenities, tourist attractions or landscape features. It is this idea of a 'useful' heritage that underpins the evaluation of archaeological remains.

Competing values

It is within a context of competing uses for the land containing archaeological remains from which Carver (1996: 47) launches his attack against current systems of evaluation (Table 6.4).

In such a formulation, archaeological value is not an absolute, nor is it primary but sits alongside other values which are hostile to

Table 6.4 Carver's (1996) competing values for land

Market values	Community values	Human values
Capital/estate value	Amenity value	Environmental value
Production value	Political value	Archaeological value
Commercial value	Minority/disadvantaged/ descendant value	
Residential value	Local style value	

and, some of them, more powerful than archaeology. Accordingly, it becomes necessary to define archaeological value in meaningful terms: for Carver this means it must be anticipatory, in the sense of being ready at the point of decision as to the future of a particular place; it must be professionally made and presented, both to document fully its content and to carry authority; and it must be able to claim the ' "global" ... character of its definition and the universal nature of its clientele and thus ... claim that it represents the interests of the largest but least influential constituency of all, that of the unborn' (Carver, 1996: 48). The objection to current systems of archaeological valuation – of 'significance' and 'importance' – is that 'behind the concerns and definitions, laws and regulations adopted by virtually all countries for the care of their "archaeological heritage" is a belief that the past is composed of "monuments" ' (Carver, 1996: 50) and it is these that are assessed under systems of archaeological heritage management. Assessment and evaluation criteria (such as those in Table 6.2) 'are designed to apply to identified sites, for which ... attributes ... can be assigned, rather than deposits which are still unseen' (Carver, 1996: 51). Accordingly, 'the concept of the monument and the ways used to define monuments contain a built-in obsolescence, because both tend to endow the future more liberally with examples of the identified, rather than the unidentified archaeological resource' (Carver, 1996: 51). His answer is to promote the research value of unknown and unassessed remains over that of value as measured in terms of 'importance', which is grounded in the already known and established.

Carver's argument is not unlike that of Schaafsma (1989) and others (e.g. Lynott, 1980; Tainter and Lucas, 1983) in certain respects and, in particular, in their focus on 'insignificance' as the only alternative to marking a site as significant. Tainter and Lucas (1983) point out that significance is not an inherent attribute of material but depends upon the context within which the judgement is being made. Accordingly – and as mentioned earlier as a factor on which all seem to agree – site significance is a dynamic and relative concept. The issue, however, is that while a designation as significant will result in preservation or investigation of the site, a failure to achieve significance may result in its loss. At the same time, and drawing on Carver's (1996) argument, significance is measured in terms of the already known rather than the yet-to-be-known. Schaafsma's (1989) answer to this is to abandon the search for 'significant' sites and instead to treat all sites as 'significant until proven otherwise'.

Throughout their arguments, Carver (1996), Schaafsma (1989) and Tainter and Lucas (1983) all emphasize that the evaluation of remains is a procedure whereby value is given by the process of evaluation rather than being inherent in the material. In taking the same line, Leone and Potter (1992) accuse CRM archaeology of both logical positivism and essentialism derived from processual styles of archaeology. Accordingly, the values placed upon archaeological material are those that relate to archaeology alone – ignoring the ways of valuing objects other people may adopt – and are accordingly fixed and static rather than contingent and relative. By adopting 'not only the "scientific rigour" and methodology of [processual archaeology] but also the authority given to archaeology by its new identity as a Science' (Smith, 1993: 58), CRM archaeology became institutionalized as a powerful discourse able to dominate the voices of others. Accordingly, to make archaeology at once more democratic and more representative of those it serves (cf. Chapter 4), Leone and Potter (1992) argue for the creation of a dialogue 'of equals' between archaeologists and others interested in a site and that the ideas of its value of both sides should be taken into consideration in the significance evaluation process. Laurajane Smith adopts a similar perspective in considering the relations between archaeologists and Aboriginal peoples in Australia (see also Chapter 5):

> The efforts by archaeologists ... to restructure archaeological philo-sophies and practices to include indigenous concerns [have] often stumbled because of the many contradictions in the way discussion of archaeological value and significance has been framed ... [A]lthough representativeness is ... not based upon neutral or objective constructs, it is nonetheless specifically employed in attempts to provide a rational assessment of the value of sites [and accordingly arguments] that archaeological ... interests are not the only legitimate interest within heritage management are often hard to make on anything more than an abstract philosophical level. Although archaeologists ... have recognised

the need to consult with Aboriginal people and other groups with ties or interests in cultural resources, these groups still argue that little *real* control is open to them. (Smith, 1996: 74)

The argument against the concept of 'significance' as conventionally applied is therefore also an argument about the role of archaeology – and the heritage more broadly – in human relations.

Heritage as 'corporate saving' in the public realm

Studies of heritage that emphasize the visitor, the tourist, the audience and the customer response to heritage sites and displays (see Chapters 4 and 5) rarely address the preceding question: why people visit such sites at all. Rare attempts to answer the question founder on the complexities of educational differences between social categories and degrees of relative poverty. Merriman's important study was able to establish that even non-visitors to heritage sites displayed an interest in the past (albeit a different one from visitors) (Merriman, 1991: 22 and 127–9) but he was unable to identify the source of that interest. This section will attempt to address that question by taking as its starting point an idea addressed in Chapter 4: that the 'public' nature of the heritage is precisely its separation from visitors and tourists. Such an idea is usually interpreted as meaning that the heritage has been appropriated from the public and put to selective use. There is, however, an alternative way of understanding this: that the heritage represents something beyond the individual and that it is not reducible to questions of individual or sectional ownership. It is, instead, a form of corporate saving by the community and such saving, as Douglas and Isherwood (1979: 37) put it, develops 'a full-fledged otherworldly morality, for the [community] outlives its members'. In drawing on ideas about value from anthropology, philosophy and sociology, a different way of valuing the archaeological heritage can be derived.

Michael Thompson and Rubbish Theory

Thompson (1979) introduces the notion that there are three categories of value into which any material may be placed: *transient* things are those of which the value is decreasing over time; *durable* things are those of which the value is increasing over time; things with no value are *rubbish* (Thompson, 1979: 7–9). At some point in their career, transient items are likely to find that their value has dropped to zero, at which point they become rubbish. Rubbish is interesting material because in general it is a category of objects deemed by cultural convention to be invisible. Rubbish consists of all the unpleasant and nasty things we do not wish to think about or to discuss and which, when we do see them, we look away from and cover our children's eyes. Those rubbish objects that force themselves onto our consciousness despite our best efforts are upsetting and dangerous. They are materials that are out of place which challenge our conceptions of how things should be arranged (Thompson, 1979: 92). This makes rubbish doubly interesting, for items that were once transient and have become rubbish can re-emerge from invisibility, challenging our assumptions about the world and forcing us to reclassify them and re-ordering our world (Thompson, 1979: 45).

Thompson's insistence on the strict application of his narrow definitions of the three value categories are important to the scheme for they determine the kinds of movement from one value-category to another that can and cannot take place (Thompson, 1979: 45). Since durable objects have a constantly increasing value, they cannot become either transient or rubbish, both of which require falling value. Transient items are decreasing in value and so can become rubbish but they cannot become durable which demands increasing value. Rubbish has no value and, accordingly, the value

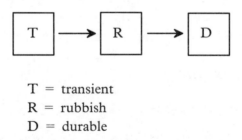

T = transient
R = rubbish
D = durable

Figure 6.1 The *Rubbish Theory* – transition to durable

cannot fall: rubbish cannot become transient objects. Transient items, however, can become rubbish since their declining value can ultimately reach zero; and rubbish which does not, by cultural convention, exist can become durable if it is manipulated and reworked to re-emerge from invisibility into our consciousness so that a new value can be placed upon it. Thompson lists several examples of this process: an old car, inner-city housing (transformed from a 'slum' to a 'period town-house' by the actions of 'Knockers Through'), Stevengraphs (a kind of Victorian kitsch decoration), and the country house at Grange Park in Hampshire (Thompson, 1979: 13–8, 19, 40–50 and 96–8).

In its delineation of transfers from one value category to another, Thompson's theory of the role of rubbish mirrors the route by which ancient remains enter the concern of the archaeologist. Schiffer (1972; 1987) outlines the process by which objects cease to be part of a 'systemic context' in the past and enter the 'archaeological context' as refuse, from which they are retrieved by archaeologists in the present. This is identical to the transition from transience to durability via rubbish delineated in *Rubbish Theory* (Carman, 1990: 196). In the past 'systemic context' objects have a transient-use value: they are made, used, re-used and disposed of. Once disposed of as 'refuse' they may be classified as rubbish; at some point they will in any case *become* rubbish in Thompson's terms since they will cease to be visible. This may be because of the physical circumstances of disposal (Schiffer's 'N-transform', by which natural processes affect the physical fabric of the object, causing it to be damaged or buried) or because of deliberate deposition in a location in which it is invisible (such as a grave) and subsequent forgetting (a 'C-transform' or cultural process) (Schiffer, 1972). The same can apply to large-scale monuments in the landscape: tales of ancient giants undertaking great building projects or the gradual acceptance of a feature as 'naturally present' rather than deliberately constructed in a human past. Once invisible and forgotten, the object is part of Thompson's *rubbish* category. On retrieval, the ancient object is given a new value in a new context. It becomes important as a means of approaching the past. This is the transition from *rubbish* to *durable*, from ancient remain to something we call 'heritage' (Carman, 1990; 1996c).

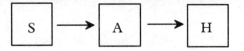

S = system (after Schiffer, 1972)
A = archaeology (after Schiffer, 1972)
H = heritage

Figure 6.2 Archaeology and *Rubbish Theory*

Jean Baudrillard and The Political Economy of the Sign

Baudrillard identifies four contemporary 'codes of value' which he designates by convenient abbreviations (Baudrillard, 1981: 125) and which, he argues, occupy spaces in the different socio-economic realms of production and consumption (Baudrillard, 1975). Use value (UV) and economic exchange value (EcEV) represent values operative in the realm of production, and also the realm of traditional political economy, where 'objects are primarily a function of needs and take on their meaning in the economic relation of man to his environment' (Baudrillard, 1981: 29). Sign exchange value (SgEV) and symbolic exchange value (SbE), however, represent values operative in the (newly emergent) realm of what he calls 'the political economy of the sign', representing 'the value of [the] *social* prestation of rivalry' which he distinguishes from that of *economic* competition (Baudrillard, 1981: 30–1, emphasis in original).

Baudrillard further identifies twelve possible conversions from one value code to another, all of them occupying spaces in one or other of these realms or providing transfer between them (Baudrillard, 1981: 123–5). Of these, only two (UV–EcEV and its reverse EcEV–UV) represent the processes of political economy – the conversion from use value to exchange value and back which is the equivalent of the 'commodity phase' in an object's life cycle (Appadurai, 1986: 15). A further conversion (UV–SbE) represents the 'promotion' of material to the symbolic realm: this includes such processes as the gift-giving of 'special' items such as engagement rings (Baudrillard, 1981: 61–9), public and official

Table 6.5 An extract from Baudrillard's conversion table of values

Value transformation	Description	Realm of activity
UV – EcEV	Use value to economic exchange value	Political economy
EcEV – UV	Economic exchange value to use value	
UV – SbE	'Promotion' to symbolic value	
SbE – UV	⎫ Return from symbolic	'Cost/benefit'
SbE – EcEV	⎬ value	analysis
SbE – SgEV	⎭	

UV = use value   SgEV = sign exchange value
EcEV = economic exchange value   SbE = symbolic exchange value

Source: Baudrillard, 1981

presentations, the potlatch and the art auction (Baudrillard, 1981: 112–22). It coincides with the notion of the promotion of items into the realm of 'heritage' as in *Rubbish Theory* (Thompson, 1979). Three further conversions (SbE–UV, SbE–EcEV and SbE–SgEV) represent the *re*conversion of symbolic value to economic/use value: this is 'the inverse of consumption: the inauguration of the economic, a "cost [benefit] analysis" of the various codes of value' (Baudrillard, 1981: 125). It will be evident from this that the conversion of values between the economic and symbolic realms and within the symbolic realm is a much more complex process than that in the economic realm, which reflects the difficulty of coming to terms with the heritage as a public phenomenon.

It is in the conversion of use value to symbolic value that heritage is created. Things promoted to a special status such that they require to be treated differently from other classes of material occupy space in the realm of symbolic value. The realm of symbolic value – that of Thompson's (1979, 103–4) 'durable – withdrawn from circulation' 'eternal object' and consequently the 'heritage' – is 'not the sanctification of a certain object. ... It is [always] the sanctification of the system [i.e. the category into which the object is placed] as such' (Baudrillard, 1981: 92). It represents a 'radical rupture' of the field of value in which all other value codes are negated (Baudrillard, 1981: 25). This is a realm of 'a generalised code of signs' (Baudrillard, 1981: 91), a *transgression* of use value' (Baudrillard, 1981: 127, emphasis in original) so that any one monument at once 'stands for' any other monument and simultaneously 'stands for' the entire class of all actual and potential monuments. This is a description of the symbolic power of the heritage as a modern 'public' phenomenon, unlike that of traditional political economy which is the antithesis of the public realm of symbolic value representing the 'private domain' of everyday life.

Pierre Bourdieu and Distinction

In criticizing Kant's philosophy of aesthetics, Bourdieu's (1984) *Distinction: A Social Critique of the Judgement of Taste* attempts to relate the kinds of material world inhabited by different classes of people in France to their social and economic position. He defines the latter in terms of various kinds of 'capital' they have acquired by birth or during their life – economic (financial), cultural, educational – and relates this to the kinds of houses they live in, the work they do, the films and music they most admire, the kind of food they eat and, finally, the newspapers they read and the politics they subscribe to. From this perspective, the two meanings of the term 'culture' ('the restricted, normative sense of ordinary usage, and ... the anthropological sense' [Bourdieu, 1984: 1]) are brought together and the appreciation of 'art' and culture generally becomes a function of social position. For Bourdieu

> the sacred sphere of culture implies an affirmation of those who can be satisfied with the ... distinguished pleasures forever closed to the profane. That is why art and cultural consumption are predisposed ... to fulfil a social function of legitimating social differences. (Bourdieu, 1984: 7)

Economic and cultural capital can be acquired in a number of ways: by birth; by gift; or by work. Together they represent aspects of one's *habitus* (or habitual way of acting in the world). Those born to wealth and privilege inherit not only economic capital in the form of money and property but frequently also a seemingly 'natural' sense of good taste and culture. Those born to the educated may inherit a sense of good taste and a knowledge of culture but not necessarily a great deal of economic capital. Those born to the rural poor are likely to inherit little of either. The process of formal education can increase the stock of cultural capital available but this acquired taste and culture is considered less worthy than that inherited at birth; the same often applies to the 'new money' wealth of the tradesperson as compared with that of the aristocrat. Least valued is the acquired cultural capital of the 'autodidact' or self-taught person, which can claim to be the product neither of birth nor of conventional formal education (Bourdieu, 1984: 85).

In the same way that some forms of personal wealth can be considered more 'worthy' than others, such as inherited versus earned wealth, so too different forms of cultural capital are often held to be more 'legitimate' than others. The two forms of capital are thus alike. Moreover, they are convertible into one another. The person with wealth can purchase a greater measure of cultural capital by taking part in expensive 'cultural' pursuits. Here, Baudrillard's designation of the art auction as a '*social* prestation of rivalry' which he distinguishes from that of a realm of strictly economic competition (Baudrillard, 1981: 30–1, emphasis in original) finds its referent. Alternatively, wealth can buy a child into a prestigious educational establishment where 'legitimate' good taste and culture can be acquired. At the same time, a high social position and its attendant stock of cultural capital which carries no financial benefit may lead to employment with high earning potential and little actual labour. While the internal dynamics of each form of capital is identical, they nevertheless represent very different material expressions; but the relations between forms of capital also allow for their mutual transformation.

Heritage values

There are certain structural similarities between all three of Thompson's and Baudrillard's ideas on value and Bourdieu's on forms of capital. Each scheme distinguishes at least two forms of their object which represent different spheres of activity. At the same time, each scheme allows the transformation of one form into another. Since the heritage is here considered as material transformed out of the 'private' realm into that of the 'public', it invites an attempt to combine these schemes into a single system which aims to say something about the heritage. Central to this combined scheme is the notion of 'promotion', since the heritage has effectively been promoted out of the everyday world into that of the abstracted and reified 'public realm'. In Thompson's scheme, 'durable' items are of higher status than 'rubbish' or the 'transient' since durable items are those with constantly increasing value. The more complex and abstract 'symbolic' realm of Baudrillard stands apart from that of economics and is the space not of competition between equals but of 'tournaments' between rivals for social status (Baudrillard, 1981: 30–1). From the perspective of cultural capital, mere economic capital represents the tawdry everyday rather than the higher appreciation of things of taste. In each case the placing of an object in the category of the durable, the symbolic or the cultural represents its 'promotion' to a higher realm. These values are equivalents in terms of the categorization of objects and represent the status given art and culture, the components of public heritage.

Cultural capital is the measure of appreciation of the symbolic value carried by the heritage, while economic capital allows the purchase of economic utility. The 'durable' and 'transient' values of *Rubbish Theory* (Thompson, 1979) equate with Baudrillard's (1981)

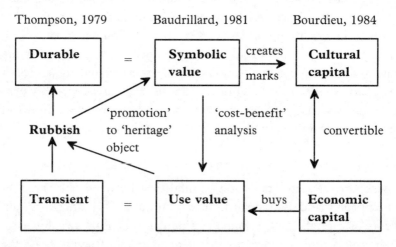

Figure 6.3 'Public' heritage values

'symbolic' and 'use' value realms and the dynamic of *Rubbish Theory* provides a model of the process by which the conversion is achieved (cf. Carman, 1990). Objects with symbolic value both mark and serve to create a stock of cultural capital, and the conversion of cultural capital to economic capital is the process by which the symbolic value of the object becomes (by Baudrillard's 'cost-benefit analysis') converted to use value which is capable of purchase. Economic capital (as financial wealth) allows the purchase of any commodity, including those with symbolic value. Here, the link between the various elements – capital and value – is access to either the capital itself or to the object carrying the appropriate value and representing the store of that capital. This extended model of the value schemes not only provides for the identical internal dynamics of each component and their mutual conversion within each scheme, but also their conversion across schemes of value. Together they provide an inkling of the qualities and the attributes of the components of the 'public' heritage to the public at large.

Beyond the value of things and back to practices

All three of the schemes of value so far covered here have one thing in common: in essence they all relate to the valuation of material objects which are the components of the heritage (cf. Chapter 2). The criticisms of each scheme in general relate to them as ways of valuing these objects – mostly either that the object is one to which it is inappropriate to ascribe a particular kind of value (such as a monetary value to museum collections) or that there is a flaw in the methodology used to calculate that value (such as the failure in assessing significance to take into account the kinds of values ascribed by the community whose heritage the object represents). Out of the discussion of each set of values arises, however, one idea which offers an alternative to them all: an abandonment of the valuation of material in favour of the valuation of practices.

'Enabling Accountability in Museums (EAM) (Carnegie and Wolnizer, 1996) shifts the focus away from the valuation of collections to the activities of institutions. Similarly, Carver's (1996) challenge to significance asserts the primacy of research value in archaeology over the 'monumental' value of preserved sites. In essence, he advocates the replacement of a 'conservation archaeology', which would establish 'archaeological preserves', with an active programme of investigation whereby 'sites of high [current] research value should be *dug*; the rest [where the current research value is low or unknown] should be *conserved*' for future research agendas (Carver, 1996: 54). The focus is thereby placed upon archaeology as an active research field, in which ideas are not fixed and static but liable to change. The idea of heritage as 'corporate saving' – although the focus is here upon conservation in perpetuity – also contains the seed of an approach based upon activity, since it emphasizes the process by which items are 'promoted' out of the usual and everyday to become heritage objects. Since archaeology is one of the fields active in creating a heritage, it is as an active force that it can be considered. The focus here shifts to the mechanisms and processes within archaeology itself which serve to identify, create and maintain the category of heritage as a separate category of material. The six practices of AHM identified in Chapter 1 – inventory, evaluation, preservation/ conservation, rescue archaeology and presentation – are capable of evaluation under schemes such as EAM. The results would not value the objects of heritage but the practices of heritage, and in turn would contribute to our own better understanding of what it is we do when we 'do' heritage.

Further reading

Giving things value

Baudrillard, J. (1981) *For a Critique of the Political Economy of the Sign*, trans. C. Levin. St Louis, MO: Telos Press.
Bourdieu, P. (1984) *Distinction: A Social Critique of the Judgement of Taste*. London: Routledge & Kegan Paul.
Douglas, M. and Isherwood, B. (1979) *The World of Goods: Towards an Anthropology of Consumption*. London: Allen Lane.
Lipe, W. (1984) 'Value and meaning in cultural resources', in H. F. Cleere (ed.) *Approaches to the Archaeological Heritage*. Cambridge: University Press, 1–11.

Thompson, M. (1979) *Rubbish Theory: The Creation and Destruction of Value*. Oxford: Clarendon.

Museums as economic institutions

Carnegie, G. D. and Wolnizer, P. M. (1996) 'Enabling accountability in museums', *Museum Management and Curatorship* **15** (4): 371–86.
Pearce, S. (ed.) (1991) *Museum Economics and the Community*. New Research in Museum Studies: an international series 2. London: Athlone Press.

Significance and its critics

Briuer, F. L. and Mathers, W. (1996) *Trends and Patterns in Cultural Resource Significance: An Historical Perspective and Annotated Bibliography*. Alexandria, VA: US Army Corps of Engineers.
Carman, J., Carnegie, G. D. and Wolnizer, P. W. (1999) 'Is archaeological valuation an accounting matter?', *Antiquity* 73: 143–8.
Carver, M. (1996) 'On archaeological value', *Antiquity*, 70: 45–56.
Darvill, T. (1995) 'Valuing archaeological resources', in M. A. Cooper *et al.* (eds) *Managing Archaeology*. London: Routledge, 40–50.
Darvill, T., Saunders, A. and Startin, B. (1987) 'A question of national importance', *Antiquity* 61: 393–408.
Leone, M. and Potter, P. B. (1992) 'Legitimation and the classification of archaeological sites', *American Antiquity* 57: 137–45.
Smith, L. (1996) 'Significance concepts in Australian management archaeology', in A. Clark and L. Smith (eds) *Issues in Management Archaeology*. St. Lucia, Queensland: Tempus Publications, University of Queensland, 67–77.
Tainter, J. A. and Lucas, J. G. (1983) 'Epistemology of the significance concept', *American Antiquity* 48: 707–19.

Summary points

1. Notions of value are central to the consideration of the purpose of creating and maintaining a set of objects set aside as 'heritage'. Differences in understanding the purpose of heritage

result in differing schemes of value, each of which draws upon a founding principle of heritage management, derives from a source discipline outside archaeology and offers a particular value scheme resulting in specific types of value.

2. The public accountability of heritage institutions can be argued to require 'transparency' in reporting procedures. By applying an accounting methodology, a financial value may be placed on a heritage object, as measured by its market value, if any, its replacement cost or how much people are prepared to pay to maintain it.

3. Since preservation of everything from the past is impossible, it becomes necessary to compare sites for their 'significance' or 'importance'. Drawing upon ideas about 'use' and 'non-use' values from economics and, possibly, by developing criteria against which to measure them, the relative merits of one site may be compared with the relative merits of other sites to ascertain the relative value of each.

4. Since the heritage as a whole is held in perpetuity as a form of 'corporate saving' for the entire community, relative valuation is meaningless. Instead, the heritage represents the community to itself and in so doing acquires an 'otherworldly morality' that exists beyond the individual.

5. Rather than focus upon valuing the material of heritage, the application of EAM, ideas about archaeology as a research field or about how the heritage is 'promoted' out of the everyday can suggest an emphasis upon heritage as a set of practices. These too are capable of measurement and evaluation, shifting attention away from the valuing of things.

Other types of heritage – the extent of the heritage field covers many other areas beyond archaeology

Plate 6.1 Literary heritage: Whiteworks, Dartmoor, Devon: inspiration for the 'Great Grimpen Mire' of Conan Doyle's *The Hound of the Baskervilles*

Plate 6.2 The heritage of social welfare and health movements: the only remaining nineteenth-century rest-house for walkers and cyclists from the industrial towns of Lancashire, England

Plate 6.3 Railway heritage: the North Yorks Steam Railway, near Whitby, North Yorkshire, England

Plate 6.4 Maritime heritage of peace: historic ships at St Katherine's Dock, London, England

Plate 6.5 Maritime heritage of war: *HMS Belfast* – the British Navy's last big-gun ship – London, England

Plate 6.6 Film heritage: one of the locations used for the Second World War action film *The Guns of Navarone*, Lindos, Greece (a past event at Lindos cited extensively in tourist literature)

Plate 6.7 Industrial heritage: disused tin mine, Bodmin Moor, Cornwall, England

Plate 6.8 Nationalist and political heritage: statue of Koloktronis, hero of the Greek War of Independence, Navplion, Greece

Plate 6.9 Global heritage of sacrifice: Tomb of the Unknown Soldier, Athens, Greece (every nation has its own Tomb of the Unknown Soldier)

Plate 6.10 Future heritage: the US Space Shuttle visiting Stansted Airport, England

Plate 6.11 Unassuming and tragic heritage: fifteenth-century home of one of the seventeenth-century 'Lancashire Witches' hanged at Lancaster Castle, Lancashire, England

Plate 6.12 Natural heritage: Table Mountain, Capetown, South Africa, from Robben Island

Plate 6.13 Varied heritage – natural, historic, industrial, political: the approach to Robben Island, Capetown, South Africa

Plate 6.14 Invisible heritage in the landscape: Koloktronis Valley, Greece – site of a Greek military victory against Ottoman rule

7 Relocating Heritage in Archaeology

This book opened with the idea that the types of theory and discourse indulged in by archaeologists were of interest and importance in considering the relationship between archaeology and heritage. In particular, readers were invited to consider what kinds of text they were reading in the field, to distinguish between the descriptive language of '*is*' and the normative language of '*should*' and to be aware of different theoretical models in application. In this final chapter, I want to pull some of these threads together in terms of the underlying themes as they have emerged in the book – especially those that appear in different guises in different chapters – and to discuss them explicitly in terms of archaeological theory and discourse. One reason for doing this is to emphasize a personal agenda, which is to encourage the consideration of the heritage field in archaeology as not only a field of practice but also as a field worthy of research in its own right. Accordingly, as suggestions to those who are inclined to take up the challenge of research, the final section of the chapter introduces an attempt to delineate areas where research could go. In particular, these include the different kinds of 'ownership' to which heritage objects are subject and the domination of the heritage by certain kinds of discourse, especially colonial and nationalist.

Heritage themes

Chapter 1 presented seven themes of heritage that would appear throughout the book: value; categorization; the 'semiotics' of objects; the aesthetics of and emotional responses to heritage; issues of otherness, alienation and commodification; the dissemination of information; and the role of archaeology and other disciplines in society. All of these themes cross-cut one another and inform other aspects of the heritage field.

Value is the sole subject of Chapter 6. However, issues of value also inform the processes whereby items are selected to become heritage objects and their treatment once so designated. In general, we assume that objects to be classed as 'heritage' already possess the characteristics and attributes of such material. One of the criticisms made of procedures for the assessment of 'significance' is that the criteria measured are held to be 'inherent' in the object rather than ascribed by the archaeologist. In fact – as noted by Briuer and Mathers (1996: 11) – all commentators agree that significance is an ascribed attribute and one that is dynamic and relative. As a bureaucratic procedure, however, it tends towards fixed criteria of measurement and standardized practices to allow comparison between objects and this can have the effect of denying its dynamic and relative nature. Such procedures also tend to leave out of account other kinds of value than those of direct relevance to the assessor. Carver's (1996) criticism of current approaches points out the emphasis placed upon known 'monumental' characteristics as opposed to future research potential in deciding which sites to preserve. Similarly, local and community values – although regarded by Carver (1996) as antithetical to archaeological values – are usually also ignored in ascribing significance (Leone and Potter, 1992). Such values – even though the local value ascribed is not directly archaeological – can also contribute to a site's research value, particularly where the site in question is part of the direct ancestral heritage of that local community (Smith, 1996). In terms of archaeological theory the distinction between a focus on exclusively archaeological values and the inclusion of local community values also has meaning: while the former generally proceeds from a 'processualist' position – generally agreed to be the foundation on which most CRM practice is built – the latter derives from positions influenced far more by post-processual or interpretive archaeologies.

The ascription of various kinds of value is also a process of categorization. Schemes of categorization were most evident in

Chapter 2, where the various kinds of heritage object were distinguished, but such schemes also underpin any procedure for taking the inventory of heritage objects (Chapter 3). In attempts to identify the archaeological 'public' (cf. McManamon, 1991; Merriman, 1991) it is inevitable that different categories of person will be created, whether distinguished functionally or on sociological grounds (Chapter 4). In establishing institutional arrangements for the management of the heritage, the distinction will be drawn between the 'public' and 'private' spheres, between levels of government and between types of institution so that, for example, 'the museum' is distinguished from 'archaeology' (Chapter 3). Categorization can be a heavily bureaucratic procedure – as in state-sponsored heritage work – but the processes of categorization are also at work in other peoples' relations to heritage. The act of distinguishing 'our' heritage from 'your' (or 'their') heritage is inevitably one of the creation of categories – not only of heritages but also of people. In responding to calls for community involvement in dealing with heritage issues, archaeologists frequently find themselves involved in deciding who has a legitimate voice and who does not. In making such decisions, it is common for those classed as 'local' and 'indigenous' to be heard (cf. Davidson *et al.*, 1995; Swidler *et al.*, 1997), whereas the voices of those classed as 'modern' and 'non-indigenous' may not (Bender, 1998: 126–30). An explicit recognition of the process of categorization at work in heritage practices tends to be a post-processual or interpretive trait; the processual approach tends to treat categorization as necessary and inevitable, which corresponds to the essentially exclusively 'archaeological' focus of processualism in general.

To categorize is also to give a meaning to things and this is very much the field of semiotics, which concerns the study of giving meaning. In line with post-processualist criticisms of processualism – that the latter in focusing on functional relations ignored the meaningful nature of human–object relations (cf. Hodder, 1992; Hodder *et al.*, 1995) – an interest in semiotics is very much part of the interpretive approach to archaeology. In creating categories, one object is set apart from other objects to which it is not deemed similar but at the same time it is compared to other objects with which it is deemed to share certain characteristics and attributes. It is in these structures of 'like' and 'unlike' that categories and objects find their value and their form. At the same time, a semiotic approach emphasizes the arbitrariness of categories: any criteria can be used to create a category and these do not have anything to do with any innate characteristics of the object to be placed in the category. But it is in the creation of categories that objects gain their meaning: whether as representing the carrying out of particular functions (as a trowel may for an archaeologist) or perhaps the cultural or other affiliations between the people whose objects they are (as a flag may indicate nationality or political affiliation). In creating categories, therefore, we give meaning to things and by arranging objects in those categories – as we may in a museum case – we present those meanings to others. These meanings require to be interpreted and we therefore need to be aware of what messages our interpretations of past material culture may deliver (Chapter 5).

Meanings are more than mere one-way messages, however: they also embody aspects of oneself and one's relations to others. As such they include our emotional responses to the world around us. In Chapter 5 it was suggested that some forms of presentation of the past may deliberately and legitimately attempt to produce particular emotional responses, aesthetic or otherwise, in their audience. In general, such forms of display are held to be antithetical to an educational or informational purpose (cf. Uzzell, 1989c; 1998). At the same time, however, highly structured and ordered bureaucratic procedures are explicitly designed to reduce the amount of subjectivity involved in decision-making and, although this cannot be entirely obliterated, it can be monitored for its effects and a degree of standardization introduced (Startin, 1993). A processual archaeology – endeavouring to produce an archaeology more scientific than humanistic in form – is also concerned to reduce or obliterate the subjective, the emotional and the political from the process of study (cf. Kohl and Fawcett, 1995). By contrast and increasingly, interpretive archaeologies seek to include the aesthetic, the subjective and the emotional in their approach (Carman and Meredith, 1990), both by attempting to appreciate the feelings of people in the past (Tarlow, 1999: 191 and 195) and by incorporating the responses of the archaeologist in the present (Bapty, 1990; Shanks, 1992; Tilley, 1994).

Those who value the inclusion of the subjective and the emotional in their dealings with the material remains of the past may levy against those who do not the charge of 'commodifying' heritage objects. The most obvious manner of doing this was discussed in Chapter 2, in terms of the international market in antiquities. However, the conversion of 'heritage' into a commodity can also be effected in other ways; Shanks and Tilley (1987) – in a review of museum displays – point out several. By focusing on the artefact as a single object in its own right, by locating it in a temporality ordained by virtue of capitalist economics, by making it an object to be gazed at and assessed aesthetically and by treating it as embodying information, the artefact becomes detached from its context and stands alone. To then put it on display – often in a manner similar to that of a shop and sometimes specifically as part of the recreation of a shop in the past – is to treat it very much as one does a commodity. This process of turning the object into a commodity can then be emphasized if the exhibit is part of an expressly commercial enterprise; and even if it is not, the mere (and standard) presence of the museum or site shop will invite consideration of objects from the past as if they are also to be bought in the shop (Shanks and Tilley, 1987, 68–99). Collections, whether private or public, are of course also a form of commodi-fication – by making the object part of a group of objects that is owned and dedicated to saying something about the owner (Chapter 2). To evaluate and assess objects – whether objects or buildings, sites, monuments or landscapes – is also to treat them as commodified entities (Shanks and Tilley, 1987: 64; Chapter 6). Such a concern with commodification – both deliberate and unforeseen – is part of a post-processual interest in locating the study of the past in its contemporary context. It extends also to a more general criticism of processual archaeology, that it supports the dominant capitalist ideology of Western societies (Yates, 1988).

The processualist answer to the charge of their commodification of the past – brought about by their treatment of and attitudes towards objects from the past - is often that archaeology is a scientific endeavour which has nothing to do with politics or economics except in terms of its expected contribution to contemporary society (cf. Schiffer, 1988). This places the focus upon heritage objects as sources of information and the purpose of archaeology then becomes the extraction and dissemination of that information. Such a perspective normalizes and justifies the conventional practices of heritage: the making of inventories, the assessment of objects, the preservation of objects, or their investigation in advance of destruction. All of these contribute towards the production of knowledge, which is the ultimate purpose of archaeology (cf. Carver, 1996). In order to fulfil its social role, it therefore becomes incumbent upon archaeologists to disseminate this information. Some of this dissemination will be to the community at large (Chapter 5). Other styles of dissemination will be more limited in scope – to clients and to colleagues in the form of professional reports or reports to national and local government agencies required by law or procedure. The processes of evaluation so central to heritage practice also involve the dissemination of information: frequently, the product of an assessment exercise will be a statement of the value of a site in terms of the attributes used to assess it. The ascription of a value in itself is also a message: it declares an object, a site or a place to be worthy of note.

In marking a place as important, archaeology also fulfils an important role: it tells us what is archaeological and – by extension, in terms of what is not so marked – what is not. This is something that all fields of activity tend to do: they mark out the space within which they operate and label the material which is theirs and, therefore, not others'. Archaeologists who work in the heritage field fulfil this necessary function for archaeology (cf. Lipe's [1984] circular process of valuation mentioned in Chapter 6). They do this by working within, for and under the authority of various institutions, including particular organizations operating at different levels (local, state, international) and under various systems of law and regulation (Chapter 3). Nevertheless, archaeology is considered an activity carried out on behalf of the public and therefore by marking certain kinds of material as belonging to the realm of archaeology archaeologists are not merely self-serving but also serve a function for society at large. Exactly what this broader social function may be is, however, frequently rather ill-defined. In general, it takes three forms: as a state-sponsored bureaucracy; as one of many different specialist professions; and as an educational and entertainment role for the community at large (Chapter 4). In this latter role it provides one of several sources for advice as to who 'we' are (depending upon how 'we' define ourselves) but also sets us standards against which to measure ourselves. One way of doing this is in terms of comparing how people may have lived in the past and how we may live now. Another is in terms of how we choose to value those things that come to us from the past, bearing in mind that one measure of civilization in modern society (however we may choose to define 'civilization') is in a concern for ancient objects.

Heritage and archaeology

Whereas Lowenthal (1996) chooses to distinguish 'heritage' from 'History' in terms of the purposes they serve and the results they achieve, one of the themes of this book is that treating archaeological remains as 'heritage' is an integral part of archaeology as a discipline. The two are therefore not considered as alternatives but are seen as components in the same field, drawing upon the same bodies of theory and disciplinary aims. Accordingly, although heritage may treat objects in one way and research in another, they can legitimately be considered to occupy different parts of the same conceptual space and to work in comparable ways on material. According to the French sociologist of knowledge Michel Foucault, the 'human sciences' are all products of modernity and exist in a conceptual realm bounded by the concerns of three previously established fields of study (Foucault, 1970, 353–4):

> *Biology*, which concerns questions of function and norms, and is thus about organising things in terms of taxonomies and categories;
> *Philology*, which concerns questions of signification and systematics and is thus about meaning and symbolic structures; and
> *Economics*, which concerns questions of conflict and rule and is thus about systems of control. (Foucault, 1970: 357)

Various approaches to branches or styles of archaeology can be located in various places in the space of Figure 7.1. Post-processual archaeology with its strong emphasis on interpretation as practice and on issues of meaning (Hodder *et al.*, 1995: 5) perhaps lies somewhere between biology and philology but, in its concern with

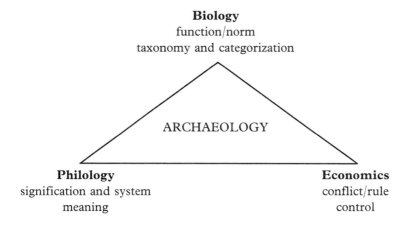

Biology
function/norm
taxonomy and categorization

ARCHAEOLOGY

Philology   **Economics**
signification and system   conflict/rule
meaning   control

Figure 7.1 Archaeology in Foucauldian space

meaning, closer to the latter. Palaeoeconomy, an approach concerned with recreating the economic aspects of past societies from environmental evidence (Higgs, 1972, 1975; Jarman *et al.*, 1982), can be located somewhere between biology and economics. Archaeological heritage management – the field to which this book contributes – can probably be placed very close to economics. And so on through all the branches of archaeology, although all three fields are implicated in all types of archaeology one way or another. On the basis of this understanding, Figure 7.1 represents a 'slice' through archaeology as a whole, with all the possible types of archaeology representing a third dimension at ninety degrees to the plane shown here. Accordingly, all styles of archaeology are involved simultaneously in questions of meaning, categorization and control – but not necessarily in that order.

From the perspective of Foucault's understanding of the human sciences, any kind of archaeological work can be seen as 'moving' the object of archaeology around in this triangular space – manipulating it. The practice of archaeology thus serves to mediate between these three areas. All archaeologists are doing the same thing, whatever label they like to stick on themselves. The only question is where do they start from and where do they end up, bearing in mind none gets outside this three-sided space?

It is in the conversion of use value to symbolic value that heritage management has its role. Heritage management starts with material

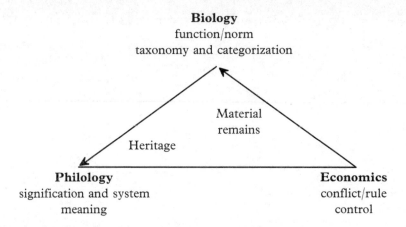

Figure 7.2 Heritage management in Foucauldian space

remains somewhere between the Biology and Economics corners of Foucault's three-sided space. These remains will finish up some-where on the other end of the base line of the triangle – in the realm of symbolic values, near the Philology corner. They do not get there directly. What happens is that the material goes through a stage of characterization and categorization (Carman, 1996c). In so doing it passes through the realm of Biology – shown here as the apex of the triangular space. Heritage management thus manipulates the object of archaeology in a particular way: it turns a material phenomenon from the past into a symbolic one in the present. Processual and post-processual archaeologies serve to manipulate it in a different way – both seek to *interpret* its place in the past (Hodder *et al.*, 1995), albeit with different purposes and results. They nevertheless operate in much the same manner, within the same conceptual space, and – as discussed in Chapter 1 – on the same material.

The political economy of the public heritage

As outlined in Chapters 3 and 4, the heritage is a public phenomenon and consists of items promoted out of the everyday world which are deemed to be valuable. The third main section of Chapter 6 offered the suggestion that the types of values carried by heritage objects are those of the 'durable' 'eternal' object, the symbolic and the cultural rather than the 'transient', utilitarian and economic. Culture is held to be durable and long-lasting and encompasses all that is common to a society or a self-affirming community. What is symbolized by the durability of shared culture is that sense of community. This reaffirms the opposition of the political to the economic and the public to the private in modernity: the symbolic value of the heritage as a public phenomenon therefore stands apart from the economic value of things in the private realm. This is one reason for the many objections to the private ownership of art objects, especially antiquities: it represents the appropriation by individuals of the shared sense of community carried by such objects. This is what is recognized by Baudrillard (1981) in his discussion of the art auction as a tournament of prestige; it is the urge that drives the antiquities market (Chapter 2) and ascribes 'esteem' to certain ancient objects classified as 'art' (Gill and Chippindale, 1993). It is also the factor recognized by Merryman in his call for a 'licit' international market in antiquities, when he points out that 'there is a close relation between art world consensus about artistic value and market value' and that these tend to change together (Merryman, 1994: 55). It is also the argument used against him, however, by those who see such objects as the legitimate property not of specific individuals but of humanity as a whole (Renfrew, 1993, 1995; Chapter 2).

The issue at stake is one of ownership. Marketable art objects and antiquities represent a store of financial value but, more importantly, they also represent other non-monetary values recognized by all concerned (Merryman 1989, 353–5). What is thus 'owned' by the acquisition of such objects is not mere financial value but also the store of symbolic and cultural value the object represents. When held by a public institution, the object's store of symbolic and cultural value serves to create and enhance the sense of community on behalf of whom the object is held. Where the object falls into private hands, that store of cultural capital accrues not to the community from which it derives but to the individual owner. Accordingly, the private ownership of cultural objects represents the appropriation of a collective cultural store of value for exclusive use. Heritage as a collective store of cultural value is not intended for private ownership; the latter represents the appropriation of a sense of community for the enhancement of an

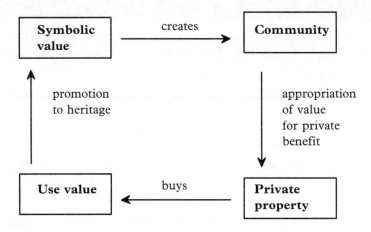

Figure 7.3 Heritage and private ownership

individual's own status, which in turn denies the very purpose of promotion of objects to 'heritage' status.

The identical principle applies in the case of the appropriation of cultural items by conquering or colonizing states from those conquered or colonized. By seizing items of symbolic 'cultural' value from another's territory and placing them in one's own, that cultural heritage accrues to the conquering or colonizing power. With it may pass a sense of identity, as in the case of the swastika symbol which imbued Nazi Germany with the full authority of an ancient Eurasian culture (Quinn, 1994). It may serve to legitimize rule, as with the transfer of 'royal' symbols to the conquering state (Greenfield, 1989: 137–53), or it may legitimize a claim to cultural continuity, as with the adoption by the Russian tsars of the imperial double-eagle of Byzantium and the acquisition by the British Museum of the Parthenon (Elgin) Marbles (Greenfield, 1989: 47–105). Here, the purpose of promoting objects to 'heritage' status is fulfilled but at the expense of the community from which such objects derive. Instead, the store of symbolic and cultural value they represent accrues to conquerors and colonizers from elsewhere.

The conventional response to the threat to the heritage of looting, private acquisitions in an international marketplace, or appropriation by aggressive outsiders is the strengthening of state controls on heritage objects. Indeed, it is conventionally held that the appropriate form of ownership for heritage objects is that of the

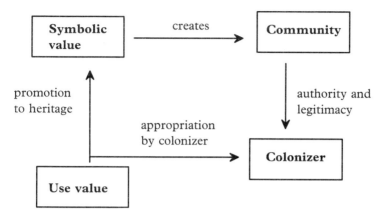

Figure 7.4 Heritage and colonial appropriation

state of origin and under international law it is inevitably states which are required to act in defence of heritage objects (Chapter 3). National laws also frequently provide for State ownership or control over heritage objects and sites. This may (as in the UK) be justified on the grounds that the role of the State is not that of exclusive owner but of guardian or custodian on behalf of the real owners, who are the wider community or 'public'. Nevertheless, what passes to the State is almost invariably either full ownership or the power to exercise ownership-style rights over the object. In this sense, the State becomes the effective owner of the object. This answer to the problem presented by looters and the market is effective but has its own consequences for the heritage which are rarely – if ever – considered.

If acquisition by private individuals or by an authority other than the state of origin of an object results in the loss of a heritage object's purpose, we should not suppose that State ownership does anything different. It is much more likely that State ownership diverts heritage value away from the collectivity of members of the community claiming affinity with the heritage object – the community itself as an 'organic' society – and towards the State as an institution. The result here is that the institution of the State – only one of a number of ways in which any society may organize itself – accrues to itself the sense of community carried by the heritage and thereby affirms its own authority as if it is the natural and only legitimate carrier of a sense of community. The symbolic value of a community's sense of heritage is converted into that of a 'national heritage' from which the nation state only can acquire prestige, in return for exercising control over that heritage. In other words, State 'ownership' of heritage does not fulfil the purposes of the heritage; instead it gives greater prestige and authority to the State as an institution. This is where we encounter the separation already discussed, of the 'public realm' as an abstracted institution in modern society from the 'public' as an agglomeration of people (Chapter 4). The connection of a heritage object – especially the symbolic and cultural durability it carries – should be made with the individual members of the community whose sense of community it represents. Instead, the connection with the heritage object is made with the political structure of the State which can then claim to legitimately represent and act on behalf of the members of that community. This connection is mediated through technologies of ownership and control which in turn serve to justify and reify the control over heritage exercised by the State.

In each of these cases the diversion of symbolic cultural value to a different purpose denies the heritage its full purpose. This denial of purpose is inevitable: the heritage is not initially created as something to be appropriated but always as something to be shared. The concept of 'my heritage' (but not yours) is a *non-sequitur* since any stock of heritage objects is always 'ours'. The only question is: who here is 'us'? In the case of private ownership, exclusivity of access denies sharing. In the case of colonial appropriation, the sharing is done by or in the name of an exclusive set of others. In the case of State-managed 'national heritage', symbolic and cultural capital accrues to the institution of the State alone. This is the condition of the archaeological heritage in modernity: a child of the division of the 'public' from the 'private' spheres of social existence, it also supports the consequent division of the 'social' and 'political' from the 'economic'. In so doing, its enhanced value is capable of return to the 'economic' realm to provide legitimizing power to appropriating institutions or persons.

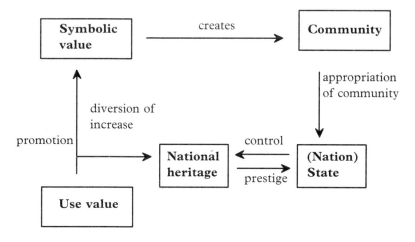

Figure 7.5 A model of national heritage

Conclusions: opening closed discourses

One of the distinguishing features of the heritage field – evident in a number of places in this book – is that it largely represents a number of 'closed' discourses. The discussion of value in Chapter 6, for example, indicated that those who subscribe to particular kinds of value scheme operate in relation to different kinds of object and in different institutions: so that a financial value may be placed upon objects in the museum but not upon monuments and sites which are the province of other – more specifically archaeological – institutions. At the same time, however, the proponents and opponents of different value schemes do not make reference to one another, so that the specifically archaeological literature (with a few exceptions) does not make reference to the ascription of a financial value to museum collections. In the same manner, those concerned with 'significance', 'importance' and similar concepts applied to monuments and sites generally do not refer either to the discussion of giving value in museums, nor to alternative schemes of heritage value. Indeed, although regarded as a matter concerning archaeology deeply, the debate over the market in movable cultural property (discussed in Chapter 2; Renfrew, 2001) has specifically not drawn upon ideas relating to the value of sites and monuments as an alternative to market value even though these ideas may be useful.

More noticeable is the tendency for discussion of heritage issues to be located within territorial boundaries (cf. Chapter 3), so that – rather than *inter*nationalizing discussion – it is a highly nationalistic discourse. As indicated in Chapter 3, most action in the heritage field is taken at the national level. Accordingly, issues of relevance to Australian heritage management will generally be limited to texts published in Australia by Australians: access to that literature by those who may face similar problems in North America will then be difficult. Similarly, the CRM literature in the USA generally fails to consider connections with other states across their territorial boundaries (although, for a bold effort to internationalize CRM debate in the Americas, see Wilson, 1988). Efforts to internationalize most often take the form of proselytizing (cf. to extend US-style CRM to Africa, see Wester, 1990; similarly Deeben *et al.*, 1999, draw upon UK and Dutch experience to offer criteria for the assessments of sites across Europe). Accordingly, one particular way of achieving a particular set of objectives will be offered to other states as a way for them to conduct their own heritage management. In such approaches a particular objective established within one national context will be deemed appropriate for others within their national context regardless of fundamental differences of history, legal system and culture. Attempts in the literature to establish a comparative approach (cf. Cleere, 1984a) generally limit themselves to a series of separate case studies based in particular territories, rather than true comparison where differences in context are taken into account so that like can be compared with like (cf. for a possible way to achieve this, Carman, 1996c: 178–83).

Most damaging to the development of the heritage field as a part of archaeology is its separation from mainstream consideration in that field. The literature of archaeological heritage management tends to be just that – the literature of a field of 'heritage' – rather than being treated as part of archaeological literature more generally. Texts on archaeological research – whether theoretical, methodological or disseminating the results of a particular project – rarely refer to heritage management aspects. Similarly, 'heritage' texts are often limited to the organizational and legal aspects of the field, ignoring archaeology as a process of research into the past. All too often, it seems in practice, Lowenthal's (1996) division is taken as necessary and inevitable.

This book has sought to begin the process of breaking down and opening up these closed discourses. By taking an explicitly international perspective – albeit limited to the English-speaking world and not all of that – it hopes to begin a shift in the way heritage is addressed in archaeology away from the national and towards the global. By being critical it has sought to open up areas to investigation previously treated as norms and to emphasize difference as an important aspect of the heritage field internationally. We do not all think the same, we do not all share the same ideas about what our heritage is composed of and we do not share common assumptions about its most appropriate treatment. This is not a weakness of the heritage field as an area of study but one of its strengths: it is what makes it interesting and exciting. But these differences – between national and disciplinary traditions, in choice of theoretical perspective, in methodology, in understandings of what archaeology is for and can offer – are also those that go to the heart of archaeology as a study of the past. The study of the 'heritage' component of archaeology, therefore, goes to the heart of archaeology itself as a discipline. That is why archaeologists in general should be concerned with heritage issues, and it thereby makes heritage the driving force in contemporary archaeology worldwide.

Suggested further reading

Locating heritage

Barrett, J. (1995) *Some Challenges in Contemporary Archaeology*. Archaeology in Britain Conference, Oxbow Lecture 2. Oxford: Oxbow.

Fowler, P. J. (1992) *The Past in Contemporary Society: Then, Now*. The Heritage: Care, Preservation, Management. London: Routledge.

Hewison, R. (1987) *The Heritage Industry: Britain in a Climate of Decline*. London: Methuen.

Hunter, M. (ed.) (1996) *Preserving the Past: The Rise of Heritage in Modern Britain*. Stroud: Sutton.

Lowenthal, D. (1985) *The Past Is a Foreign Country*. Cambridge: Cambridge University Press.

Lowenthal, D. (1996) *The Heritage Crusade and the Spoils of History*. London: Viking.

Walsh, K. (1992) *The Representation of the Past: Museums and Heritage in the Post-modern World*. The Heritage: Care, Preservation, Management. London, Routledge.

Wright, P. (1985) *On Living in an Old Country*. London: Verso.

Archaeology and relations of power

Bond, G. C. and Gilliam, A. (eds) (1994) *The Social Construction of the Past: Representation as Power*. London: Routledge.

Diaz-Andreu, M. and Champion, T. (eds) (1996) *Nationalism and Archaeology in Europe*. London: Routledge.

Jones, S. (1997) *The Archaeology of Ethnicity: Constructing Identities in the Past and Present*. London: Routledge.

Kohl, P. L. and Fawcett, C. (eds) (1995) *Nationalism, Politics and the Practice of Archaeology*. Cambridge: Cambridge University Press.

McGuire, R. H. and Paynter, R. (eds) (1991) *The Archaeology of Inequality*. Oxford: Blackwell.

Meskell, L. (1998) *Archaeology under Fire: Nationalism, Politics and Heritage in the Eastern Mediterranean and Middle East*. London: Routledge.

Miller, D., Rowlands, M. and Tilley, C. (eds) (1989) *Domination and Resistance*. One World Archaeology 3. London: Routledge.

Trigger, B. G. (1984) 'Alternative archaeologies: nationalist, colonialist, imperialist', *Man* 19: 355–70.

Summary points

1. Although it is possible to separate out individual themes which dominate the field of heritage, these themes are in themselves complex and interlocking. None can be entirely divorced from its impact on other aspects of heritage.

2. Heritage themes also relate directly to issues more directly implicated in the practice of archaeology as a research field. Accordingly, the approach taken to a particular issue in the field of heritage and its management will both reflect and derive from positions relating to ideas about how archaeology should be done and what the purpose of archaeology should be.

3. Although often treated as a field separate from archaeology – either as a sub-discipline or as a separate field altogether – a strong case can be made for their unity. In particular, they concern the manner of treating identical bodies of material and can be understood to do so within the same conceptual space.

4. Issues of ownership suffuse the heritage field and can be used as a means to understand some of its complexities. In particular, ideas about ownership are dominant themes in issues of private ownership, colonial appropriation and nationalism in relation to heritage and each also leads us back to a concern with different kinds of value. Here, the interlocking of heritage themes is at once evident but it also provides an issue amenable to research in its own right.

5. Heritage represents a field of 'closed' discourses in which heritage is separated from its host disciplines of archaeology and history, discussion takes place within territorial boundaries rather than being effectively internationalized, and those who subscribe to different schemes of value do not exchange perspectives. The way forward for heritage is to open these closed discourses to globalize the debate and to reforge the close links with host disciplines for mutual benefit.

References

Aberg, F. A. and Leech, R. H. (1992) 'The National Archaeological Record in England: past, present and future', in National Museum of Denmark, *Sites and Monuments: National Archaeological Records*. Copenhagen: National Museum of Denmark, 157–70.

Adovaiso, J. M. and Carlisle, R. C. (1988) 'Some thoughts on cultural resource management archaeology in the United States', *Antiquity* 62: 72–87.

Albrow, M. (1970) *Bureaucracy*. London: Pall Mall Press.

Aldridge, D. (1989) 'How the ship of interpretation was blown off course in the tempest: some philosophical thoughts', in D. Uzzell (ed.) *Heritage Interpretation: Volume 1. The Natural and Built Environment*. London: Bellhaven, 64–87.

Allen, M. (1995) *Altamira's Rules for the Archaelogical Writer*, Walnut Creek, CA: Altamira Press.

Ames, P. J. (1994) 'Measuring museums' merits', in K. Moore (ed.) *Museum Management*. Leicester Readers in Museum Studies. London: Routledge, 22–30.

Andah, B. W. (ed.) (1990) 'Cultural resource management: an African dimension', Forum on Cultural Resource Management at the Conference in Honour of Professor Thurstan Shaw, *West African Archaeology* 20.

Appadurai, A. (1986) 'Introduction: commodities and the politics of value', in A. Appadurai (ed.) *The Social Life of Things: Commodities in Cultural Perspective*. Cambridge: Cambridge University Press, 3–63.

Archaeologia Polona (2000) 'Archaeological heritage management: theory and practice', *Archaeologia Polona* 38.

Ardouin, C. D. (ed.) (1997) *Museums and Archaeology in West Africa*. Oxford and Washington, DC: James Currey and Smithsonian Institution Press.

Ascherson, N. (2000) Editorial, *Public Archaeology* 1: 1–4.

Backschieder, P. and Dykstal, T. (eds) (1996) *The Intersections of the Public and Private Spheres in Early Modern England*. London: Frank Cass.

Ballantyne, R. and Uzzell, D. (1993) 'Environmental mediation and hot interpretation: a case study of District Six, Capetown', *Journal of Environmental Education* 24 (3): 4–7.

Bapty, I. (1990) 'The Agony and the Ecstasy: the emotions of writing the past', *Archaeological Review from Cambridge* **9** (2): 233–42.

Bapty, I. and Yates, T. (eds) (1990) *Archaeology after Structuralism: Poststructuralism and the Practice of Archaeology*. London: Routledge.

Barrett, J. (1987) 'Fields of discourse: reconstituting a social archaeology', *Critique of Anthropology* **7** (3): 5–16.

Barrett, J. (1994) *Fragments from Antiquity: An Archaeology of Social Life in Britain 2900–1200 BC*. Oxford: Blackwell.

Barrett, J. (1995) *Some Challenges in Contemporary Archaeology*. Archaeology in Britain Conference, Oxbow Lecture 2. Oxford: Oxbow.

Barrett, J., Bradley, R., and Green, M. (1991) *Landscape, Monuments and Society: The Prehistory of Cranborne Chase*. Cambridge: Cambridge University Press.

Baudrillard, J. (1975) *The Mirror of Production*, trans. M. Poster. St Louis, MO: Telos Press.

Baudrillard, J. (1981) *For a Critique of the Political Economy of the Sign*, trans. C. Levin. St Louis, MO: Telos Press.

Belcher, M. (1991) *Exhibitions in Museums*. Leicester: Leicester University Press.

Bender, B. (1993) 'Introduction – landscape – meaning and action', in B. Bender (ed.) *Landscape – Politics and Perspectives*. Oxford: Berg, 1–17.

Bender, B. (1998) *Stonehenge: Making Space*. Oxford: Berg.

Benn, S. I. and Gaus, G. F. (1983a) 'The liberal conception of the public and the private', in S. I. Benn and G. F. Gaus (eds) *Public and Private in Social Life*. London: Croom Helm, 31–65.

Benn, S. I. and Gaus, G. F. (1983b) 'The public and the private: concepts and action', in S. I. Benn and G. F. Gaus (eds) *Public and Private in Social Life*. London: Croom Helm, 3–27.

Berger, P. (1973) *The Homeless Mind*. Harmondsworth: Penguin.

Biddle, M. (1989) '*The Rose* reviewed: a comedy(?) of errors', *Antiquity* 63: 753–60.

Binford, L. (ed.) (1977) *For Theory Building in Archaeology: Essays on Faunal Remains, Aquatic Resources, Spatial Analysis and Systematic Modelling*. Studies in Archaeology. New York: Academic Press.

Binford, L. (1983) *Working at Archaeology*. Studies in Archaeology. San Diego: Academic Press.

Binford, L. (1989) *Debating Archaeology*. Studies in Archaeology. San Diego: Academic Press.

Blau, P. M. (1956) *Bureaucracy in Modern Society*. New York: Random House.

Bold, J. and Chaney, E. (eds) (1993) *English Architecture: Public and Private: Essays for Kerry Downes*. London: Hambledon Press.

Bond, G. C. and Gilliam, A. (eds) (1994) *The Social Construction of the Past: Representation as Power*. London: Routledge.

Boniface, P. and Fowler, P. J. (1993) *Heritage and Tourism in 'The Global Village'*. London: Routledge.

Bourdieu, P. (1984) *Distinction: A Social Critique of the Judgement of Taste*. London: RKP.

Boylan, P. (ed.) (1992) *Museums 2000: Politics, People, Professionals and Profit*. London: Routledge.

Brawe, M. 1965. *The New Museum: Architecture on Display*. London: Architectural Press.

Brisbane, M. and Wood, J. (1996) *A Future for Our Past? An Introduction to Heritage Studies*. London: English Heritage.

Brown, A. E. (1991) *Garden Archaeology*. CBA Research Report 78. London: CBA.

Briuer, F. L. and Mathers, W. (1996) *Trends and Patterns in Cultural Resource Significance: An Historical Perspective and Annotated Bibliography*. Alexandria, VA: US Army Corps of Engineers.

Butzer, K. W. (1982) *Archaeology as Human Ecology: Method and Theory for a Contextual Approach*. Cambridge: Cambridge University Press.

Byrne, D. (1991) 'Western hegemony in archaeological heritage management', *History and Anthropology* 5: 269–76.

Cannon-Brookes, P. (1994) 'Antiquities in the market-place: placing a price on documentation', *Antiquity* 68: 349–50.

Canouts, V. (1992) 'Computerised information exchange on the local and national levels in USA', in National Museum of Denmark, *Sites and Monuments: National Archaeological Records*. Copenhagen: National Museum of Denmark, 231–47.

Carman, J. (1990) 'Commodities, rubbish and treasure: valuing archaeological objects', *Archaeological Review from Cambridge* 9 (2): 195–207.

Carman, J. (1993) 'The P is silent – as in archaeology', *Archaeological Review from Cambridge* 12 (1): 39–53.

Carman, J. (1995) 'Interpretation, writing and presenting the past', in I. Hodder, M. Shanks, A. Alexandri, V. Buchli, J. Carman, J. Last and G. Lucas (eds) *Interpreting Archaeology: Finding Meaning in the Past*. London: Routledge, 95–9.

Carman, J. (1996a) 'Data for the future or an amenity for the present: the values of the historic and natural wetland environment', in M. Cox, V. Straker and D. Taylor (eds) *Wetlands: Archaeology and Nature Conservation*. London: HMSO, 18–29.

Carman, J. (1996b) 'Unfolding museums: storylines for the future', *Museological Review* 2 (1): 1–20.

Carman, J. (1996c) *Valuing Ancient Things: Archaeology and Law*. London: Leicester University Press.

Carman, J. (1998) 'Object values: landscapes and their contents', in M. Jones and D. Rotherham (eds) *Landscapes – Perception, Recognition and Management: Reconciling the Impossible? Landscape Archaeology and Ecology* 2. Sheffield: Landscape Conservation Forum, 31–4.

Carman, J. (1999a) 'Beyond the western way of war: ancient battlefields in comparative perspective', in J. Carman and A. Harding (eds) *Ancient Warfare: Archaeological Perspectives*. Stroud: Sutton, 39–55.

Carman, J. (1999b) 'Bloody Meadows: the places of battle', in S. Tarlow and S. West (eds) *The Familiar Past? Archaeologies of Later Historical Britain*. London: Routledge, 233–45.

Carman, J. (1999c) 'Settling on sites: constraining concepts', in J. M. Brück and M. Goodman (eds) *Making Places in the Prehistoric World: Themes in Settlement Archaeology*. London: UCL Press, 20–9.

Carman, J. (2000) 'Theorising the practice of archaeological heritage management', *Archaeologia Polona* 38: 5–21.

Carman, J., Carnegie, G. D. and Wolnizer, P. W. (1999) 'Is archaeological valuation an accounting matter?', *Antiquity* 73: 143–8.

Carman, J. and Meredith. J. (eds) (1990) '*Affective archaeology*', *Archaeological Review from Cambridge* 9.2.

Carmichael, D. L., Hubert, J., Reeves, B. and Schanche, A. (eds) (1994) S*acred Sites, Sacred Places*. London: Routledge.

Carnegie, G. D. and Wolnizer, P. M. (1995) 'The financial value of cultural, heritage and scientific collections: an accounting fiction', *Australian Accounting Review* 5 (1): 31–47.

Carnegie, G. D. and Wolnizer, P. M. (1996) 'Enabling accountability in museums', *Museum Management & Curatorship* 15 (4): 371–86.

Carnegie, G. D. and Wolnizer, P. M. (1999) 'Unravelling the rhetoric about the financial reporting of public collections as assets: a response to Micallef and Peirson', *Australian Accounting Review* 9 (1): 16–21.

Carver, M. (1996) 'On archaeological value', *Antiquity* 70:45–56.

Chippindale, C. and Taçon, P. (1998) *The Archaeology of Rock-art*. Cambridge: Cambridge University Press.

Clark, K. (forthcoming) 'Robben Island – a political landscape at risk', in J. Schofield, W. G. Johnson and C. Beck (eds) *Matériel Culture: The Archaeology of 20th Century Conflict*. London: Routledge.

Clarke, D. L. (1968) *Analytical Archaeology*. London: Methuen.

Cleere, H. F. (ed.) (1984a) *Approaches to the Archaeological Heritage*. Cambridge: Cambridge University Press.

Cleere, H. F. (1984b) 'Great Britain', in H. F. Cleere (ed.) *Approaches to the Archaeological Heritage*. Cambridge: Cambridge University Press, 54–62.

Cleere, H. F. (1984c) 'World cultural resource management: problems and perspectives', in H. F. Cleere (ed.) *Approaches to the Archaeological Heritage*. Cambridge: Cambridge University Press, 125–31.

Cleere, H. F. (ed.) (1989) *Archaeological Heritage Management in the Modern World*. London: Unwin Hyman.

Clifford, J. (1988) *The Predicament of Culture: Twentieth-century Ethnography, Literature and Art*. Cambridge, MA: Harvard University Press.

Cook, B. F. (1991) 'The archaeologist and the art market: policies and practice', *Antiquity* 65: 533–7.

Cooper, M. A., Firth, A., Carman, J. and Wheatley, D. (eds) (1995) *Managing Archaeology*. TAG. London: Routledge.

Countryside Commission (1989) *A People's Charter: Forty Years of the National Parks and Access to the Countryside Act 1949*. London: HMSO.

Crowther, D. (1989) 'Archaeology, material culture and museums', in S. M. Pearce (ed.) *Museum Studies in Material Culture*. Leicester: Leicester University Press, 35–46.

Daniel, G. and Renfrew, C. (1988) *The Idea of Prehistory*. Edinburgh: Edinburgh University Press.

Darvill, T. (1987) *Ancient Monuments in the Countryside: An Archaeological Management Review*. English Heritage Archaeological Report 5. London: English Heritage.

Darvill, T. (1993) *Valuing Britain's Archaeological Resource*. Bournemouth University Inaugural Lecture. Bournemouth: Bournemouth University.

Darvill, T. (1995) 'Value systems in archaeology', in M. A. Cooper, A. Firth, J. Carman and D. Wheatley (eds) *Managing Archaeology*. London: Routledge, 40–50.

Darvill, T. (1996) 'Landscapes: myth or reality?', in M. Jones and D. Rotherham (eds) *Landscapes – Perception, Recognition and Management: Reconciling the Impossible? Landscape Archaeology and Ecology* 2. Sheffield: Landscape Conservation Forum, 11–13.

Darvill, T., Gerrard, G. and Startin, B. (1993) 'Identifying and protecting historic landscapes', *Antiquity* 67: 563–74.

Darvill, T., Saunders, A. and Startin, B. (1987) 'A question of national importance: approaches to the evaluation of ancient monuments for the Monuments Protection Programme in England', *Antiquity* 61: 393–408.

Davidson, I., Lovell-Jones, C. and Bancroft, R. (eds) (1995) *Archaeologists and Aborigines Working Together*. Armidale: University of New England Press.

Deeben, J., Groenewoudt, B. J., Hallewas, D. P. and Willems, W. J. H. (1999) 'Proposals for a practical system of significance evaluation in archaeological heritage management', *European Journal of Archaeology* 2 (2): 177–200.

Department of the Environment (1990) *Archaeology and Planning: Planning Policy Guideline Note No. 16*. London: Department of the Environment, November 1990.

Diaz-Andreu, M. and Champion, T. (eds) (1996) *Nationalism and Archaeology in Europe*. London: Routledge.

Douglas. M. (1987) *How Institutions Think*. London: RKP.

Douglas, M. and Isherwood, B. (1979) *The World of Goods: Towards an Anthropology of Consumption*. London: Allen Lane.

Dunnell, R. C. (1984) 'The ethics of archaeological significance decisions', in Green, E. L. (ed.) *Ethics and Values in Archaeology*. New York: Free Press, 62–74.

Dunnell, R. C. (1992) 'The notion site', in J. Rossignol and L. Wandsnider (eds) *Space, Time and Archaeological Landscapes*. New York: Plenum Press, 21–41.

Edson, G. and Dean. D. (1994) *The Handbook for Museums*. London: Routledge .

English Heritage (1988) *Visitors Welcome! A Manual on the Presentation and Interpretation of Archaeological Remains*. London: English Heritage.

English Heritage (1991) *Managing Archaeological Projects (MAP2)*. London: English Heritage.

Ennen. E. (2000) 'The meaning of heritage according to connoisseurs, rejecters and take-it-or-leavers in historic city centres: two Dutch cities experienced', *International Journal of Heritage Studies* **6** (4): 331–50.

Faulkner, N. (2000) 'Archaeology from below', *Public Archaeology* 1, 21–33.

Field, J., Barker, J., Barker, R., Coffey, E., Coffey, L., Crawford, E., Darcy, L., Fields, T., Lord, G., Steadman, B. and Colley, S. (2000) ' "Coming back": Aborigines and archaeologists at Cuddie Springs', *Public Archaeology* 1: 35–48.

Firth, A. (1993) 'The management of archaeology underwater', in J. Hunter and I. Ralston (eds) *Archaeological Resource Management in the UK: An Introduction*. Stroud: Sutton, 65–76.

Firth, A. (1995) 'Ghosts in the machine', in M. A. Cooper, J. Carman, A. Firth and D. Wheatley (eds) *Managing Archaeology*. London: Routledge, 51–67.

Foucault, M. (1970) *The Order of Things: An Archaeology of the Human Sciences*. London: Tavistock.

Foucault, M. (1972) *The Archaeology of Knowledge and the Discourse on Language*. London: Tavistock.

Foucault, M. (1977) *Discipline and Punish: The Birth of the Prison*, French edition (1975) entitled *Surveiller et punir: naissance de la prison*, trans. A. Sheridan. London: Allen Lane.

Fourmile, H. (1996) 'The law of the land: whose law? whose land?', in A. Clark and L. Smith (eds) *Issues in Management Archaeology*. St. Lucia, Qld: Tempus Publications, University of Queensland, 45–50.

Fowler, D. D. (1982) Cultural resources management', in M. B. Schiffer (ed.) *Advances in Archaeological Method and Theory* 5. San Diego: Academic Press, 1–50.

Fowler, D. D. (1984) 'Ethics in contract archaeology', in E. L. Green (ed.) *Ethics and Values in Archaeology*. New York: Free Press, 108–16.

Fowler, P. J. (1992) *The Past in Contemporary Society: Then, Now*. The Heritage: Care, Preservation, Management. London: Routledge.

Fowler, P. J. (1995) 'Writing on the countryside', in I. Hodder, M. Shanks, A. Alexandri, V. Buchli, J. Carman, J. Last and G. Lucas (eds) *Interpreting Archaeology: Finding Meaning in the Past*. London: Routledge, 100–109.

Fraser, D. (1993) 'The British archaeological database', in J. Hunter and I. Ralston (eds) *Archaeological Resource Management in the UK: An Introduction*. Stroud: Sutton, 19–29.

Freeman, P. and Pollard, T. (eds) (2001) *Fields of Conflict: Progress and Prospects in Battlefield Archaeology*. Oxford: BAR.

Fukayama, F. (1992) *The End of History and the Last Man*. London: Hamish Hamilton.

Gavison, R. (1983) 'Information control: availability and exclusion', in S. I. Benn and G. F. Gaus (eds) *Public and Private in Social Life*. London: Croom Helm, 113–34.

Gell, A. (1986) 'Newcomers to the world of goods: the Muria Gonds', in A. Appadurai (ed.) *The Social Life of Things: Commodities in Cultural Perspective*. Cambridge: Cambridge University Press, 110–38.

Giddens, A. (1984) *The Constitution of Society: Outline of the Theory of Structuration*. Cambridge: Polity Press.

Gill, D. and Chippindale, C. (1993) 'Material and intellectual consequences of esteem for Cycladic figures', *American Journal of Archaeology* **97** (3): 602–73.

Gould, S. (1998) 'Planning, development and Social Archaeology', in S. Tarlow and S. West (eds) *The Familiar Past? Archaeologies of Later Historical Britain*. London: Routledge.

Gould, R. A. and Schiffer, M. B. (eds) (1981) *Modern Material Culture: The Archaeology of Us*. Studies in Archaeology. New York: Academic Press.

Greenfield, J. (1989) *The Return of Cultural Treasures*. Cambridge: Cambridge University Press.

Gurr, A. (1994) 'Static scenes at the Globe and the Rose Elizabethan theatres', *Antiquity* 68: 146–7.

Harris, E. C. (1979) *Principles of Archaeological Stratigraphy*. London: Academic Press.

Heath, M. A. (1997) 'Successfully integrating the public into research: Crow Canyon Archaeology Center', in J. H. Jameson (ed.) *Presenting Archaeology to the Public: Digging for Truths*. Walnut Creek, CA: Altamira Press, 65–72.

Helly, D. O. and Reverby, S. M. (eds) (1992) *Gendered Domains: Rethinking Public and Private in Women's History: Essays from the Seventh Berkshire Conference on the History of Women*. Ithaca, NY: Cornell University Press.

Herzfeld, M. (1991) *A Place in History: Social and Monumental Time in a Cretan Town*. Princeton, NJ, and Oxford: Princeton University Press.

Herzfeld, M. (1992) *The Social Production of Indifference: Exploring the Symbolic Roots of Western Bureaucracy*. Chicago: University of Chicago Press. .

Herzfeld, M. (1997) *Cultural Intimacy: Social Poetics in the Nation State*. London: Routledge.

Hewison, R. (1987) *The Heritage Industry: Britain in a Climate of Decline*. London: Methuen.

Higgs, E. S. (ed.) (1972) *Papers in Economic Prehistory*. Cambridge: Cambridge University Press.

Higgs, E. S. (ed.) (1975) *Palaeoeconomy*. Cambridge: Cambridge University Press.

Hill, Sir G. (1936) *Treasure Trove in Law and Practice from the Earliest Time to the Present Day*. Oxford: Clarendon.

Hodder, I. (1982) *Symbols in Action: Ethnoarchaeological Studies of Material Culture*. New Studies in Archaeology. Cambridge: Cambridge University Press.

Hodder, I. (1986) *Reading the Past: Current Approaches to Interpretation in Archaeology*. Cambridge: Cambridge University Press.

Hodder, I. (1989) 'Postmodernism, post-structuralism and post-processual archaeology', in I. Hodder (ed.) *The Meanings of Things: Material Culture and Symbolic Expression*. One World Archaeology 6. London: Unwin Hyman, 64–78.

Hodder, I. (1992) *Reading the Past: Current Approaches to Interpretation in Archaeology* (2nd edition). Cambridge: Cambridge University Press.

Hodder, I. (1999) *The Archaeological Process*. Oxford: Blackwell.

Hodder, I. and Preucel, R. (1996) *Contemporary Archaeology in Theory: A Reader*. Cambridge, MA: Blackwell.

Hodder, I., Shanks, M., Alexandri, A., Buchli, V., Carman, J., Last, J. and Lucas, G. (eds) (1995) *Interpreting Archaeology: Finding Meaning in the Past*. London: Routledge.

Hoffman, T. L. (1997) 'The role of public participation: Arizona's public archaeology program', in J. H. Jameson (ed.) *Presenting Archaeology to the Public: Digging for Truths*. Walnut Creek, CA: Altamira Press, 73–83.

Holtorf, C. (2001) 'Sculptures in captivity and monkeys on megaliths: observations in zoo archaeology', *Public Archaeology* 1: 195–200.

Holtorf, C. and Schadla-Hall, T. (2000) 'Age as artefact', *European Journal of Archaeology* 2 (2): 229–48.

Hone, P. (1997) 'The financial value of cultural, heritage and scientific collections: a public management necessity', *Australian Accounting Review* 7 (1): 38–43.

Hubert, J. (1989) 'A proper place for the dead: a critical review of the "reburial" issue', in R. Layton (ed.) *Conflict in the Archaeology of Living Traditions*. London: Routledge, 131–66.

Hunter, J. and Ralston I. (eds) (1993) *Archaeological Resource Management in the UK: An Introduction*. Stroud: Sutton.

Hunter, M. (ed.) (1996) *Preserving the Past: The Rise of Heritage in Modern Britain*. Stroud: Sutton.

ICOM (International Council of Museums) (1989) 'Definitions', *Code of Professional Ethics*. Paris: ICOM, 23.

Isler-Kerényi, C. (1994) 'Are collectors the real looters?', *Antiquity* 68: 350–2.

Jarman, M. R., Bailey, G. N. and Jarman, H. N. (eds) (1982) *Early European Agriculture: Its Foundation and Development*. Cambridge: Cambridge University Press.

Jameson, J. H. (ed.) (1997) *Presenting Archaeology to the Public: Digging for Truths*. Walnut Creek, CA: Altamira Press.

Johnson, B. (1996) 'Nature conservation and archaeology: English Nature's lowland peatland programme', in M. Cox, V. Straker and D. Taylor (eds) *Wetlands: Archaeology and Nature Conservation*. London: HMSO.

Johnson, M. (1993) *Housing Culture: Traditional Architecture in an English Landscape*. London: UCL Press.

Johnson, M. (1999) *Archaeological Theory: An Introduction*. Oxford: Blackwell.

Johnson, P. and Thomas, B. (1991) 'Museums: an economic perspective', in S. Pearce (ed.) *Museum Economics and the Community*. New Research in Museum Studies: an international series 2. London: Athlone Press, 5–40.

Jones, M. and Rotherham, D. (eds) (1998) *Landscapes – Perception, Recognition and Management: Reconciling the Impossible? Landscape Archaeology and Ecology* 2. Sheffield: Landscape Conservation Forum.

Jones, S. (1997) *The Archaeology of Ethnicity: Constructing Identities in the Past and Present*. London: Routledge.

King, T. F., Hickman, P. P., and Berg, G. (1977) *Anthropology in Historic Preservation: Caring for Culture's Clutter*. Studies in Archaeology. New York: Academic Press.

Kohl, P. L. and Fawcett, C. (eds) (1995) *Nationalism, Politics and the Practice of Archaeology*. Cambridge: Cambridge University Press.

Landry, C. (1994) 'Measuring the viability and vitality of city centres', in C. Mercer (ed.) *Urban and Regional Quality of Life Indicators*. Brisbane: Griffith University Institute of Cultural Policy Studies, 13–32.

Layton, R. (ed.) (1989a) *Conflict in the Archaeology of Living Traditions*. London: Routledge.

Layton, R. (ed.) (1989b) *Who Needs the Past? Indigenous Values and Archaeology*. London: Routledge.

Lee Long, D. (2000) 'Cultural heritage management in post-colonial polities: *not* the heritage of the other', *International Journal of Heritage Studies* **6** (4): 317–22.

Leone, M. (1984) 'Interpreting archaeology in historical archaeology: the William Paca garden, in Annapolis', in D. Miller and C. Tilley (eds) *Ideology, Power and Prehistory*. Cambridge: Cambridge University Press, 25–36.

Leone, M. and Potter, P. B. (1992) 'Legitimation and the classification of archaeological sites', *American Antiquity* 57: 137–45.

Leone, M. P., Mullins, P. R., Creveling, C., Hurst, L., Jackson-Nash, B., Jones, L. D., Kaiser, H. J., Logan, G. C. and Warner, M. S. (1995) 'Can an African-American historical archaeology be an alternative voice?', in I. Hodder, M. Shanks, A. Alexandri, V. Buchli, J. Carman, J. Last and G. Lucas (eds) *Interpreting Archaeology: Finding Meaning in the Past*. London: Routledge, 110–24.

Leone, M., Potter, P. B. and Shackel, P. A. (1987) 'Toward a critical archaeology', *Current Anthropology* 57 (1): 137–45.

Lipe, W. D. (1974) 'A conservation model for American archaeology', *The*

Kiva 39 (3–4): 213–45.

Lipe, W. D. (1984) 'Value and meaning in cultural resources', in H. F. Cleere (ed.) *Approaches to the Archaeological Heritage*. Cambridge: Cambridge University Press, 1–11.

Lowenthal, D. (1985) *The Past Is a Foreign Country*. Cambridge: Cambridge University Press.

Lowenthal, D. (1996) *The Heritage Crusade and the Spoils of History*. London: Viking.

Lucas, G. (2001) *Critical Approaches to Fieldwork: Contemporary and Historical Archaeological Practice*. London: Routledge.

Lynott, M. J. (1980) 'The dynamics of significance: an example from central Texas', *American Antiquity* 45 (1): 117–20.

Martin, F. (1994) 'Determining the size of museum subsidies', *Journal of Cultural Economics* 18: 255–70.

Mathers, C., Darvill, T. and Little, B. (eds) (forthcoming) *Archaeological Assessment and Significance*. Westport, CT: Greenwood Press.

Mbunwe-Samba, P. (1989) 'Oral traditions and the African past', in R. Layton (ed.) *Who Needs the Past?* London: Unwin Hyman, 105–18.

McDavid, C. (1997) 'Descendants, decisions and power: the public interpretation of the archaeology of the Levi Jordan plantation', in C. McDavid and D. Babson (eds) *In the Realm of Politics: Prospects for Public Participation in African-American Archaeology*. California: Society for Historical Archaeology (= *Historical Archaeology* 31 [3]), 114–31.

McDavid, C.(1999) 'From real space to cyberspace: contemporary conversations about the archaeology of slavery and tenancy', *Internet Archaeology* 6, Special Theme: *Digital Publication*, http://intarch.ac.uk/journal/issue6/mcdavid_toc.html. Updated May 1999, accessed 12 April 2001.

McDavid, C. (2000) 'Archaeology as cultural critique: pragmatism and the archaeology of a southern states plantation', in C. Holtorf and H. Karlsson (eds) *Philosophy and Archaeological Practice: Perspectives for the 21st Century*. Göterborg: Göterborg Institutionen för Arkeologi.

McDavid C. (forthcoming) 'Towards a more democratic archaeology? The internet and public archaeological practice', in N. Merriman and T. Schadla-Hall (eds) *Public Archaeology*. London: Routledge.

McDavid, C. and Babson, D. (eds) (1997) *In the Realm of Politics: Prospects for Public Participation in African-American Archaeology*. California: Society for Historical Archaeology (= *Historical Archaeology* 31: 3).

McDonald, J. D., Zimmerman, L. J., McDonald, A. L., Tall Bull, W. and Rising Sun, T. (1991) 'The Northern Cheyenne outbreak of 1879: using oral history and archaeology as tools of resistance', in R. H. McGuire and R. Paynter (eds) *The Archaeology of Inequality*. Oxford: Blackwell, 64–78.

McGimsey, C. R. (1972) *Public Archaeology*. New York: Seminar Books.

McGimsey, C. R. (1984) 'The value of archaeology', in E. L. Green (ed.) *Ethics and Values in Archaeology*. New York: Free Press, 171–4.

McGimsey, C. R. and Davis, H. R. (eds) (1977) *The Management of Archaeological Resources: The Airlie House Report*. Washington, DC: Society for American Archaeology.

McGuire, R. H. and Paynter, R. (eds) (1991) *The Archaeology of Inequality*. Oxford: Blackwell.

McKinley, J. R. and Jones, R. (eds) (1979) *Archaeological Resource Management in Australia and Oceana*. Wellington, NZ: New Zealand Historic Places Trust.

McManamon, F. P. (1991) 'The many publics for archaeology', *American Antiquity* 56: 121–30.

McManamon, F. P. (2000) 'Archaeological messages and messengers', *Public Archaeology* 1: 5–20.

McSweeney, B. (1997) 'The unbearable ambiguity of accounting', *Accounting, Organizations and Society* 22 (7): 691–712.

Mehrabian, A. (1976) *Public Places and Private Spaces: The Psychology of Work, Play and Living Environments*. New York: Basic Books.

Merriman, N. (1989) 'Museum visiting as a cultural phenomenon', in P. Vergo (ed.) *The New Museology*. London: Reaktion Books, 149–71.

Merriman, N. (1991) *Beyond the Glass Case: The Public, Museums and Heritage in Britain*. London: Leicester University Press.

Merryman, J. (1989) 'The public interest in cultural property', *California Law Review* 77 (2): 339–64.

Merryman, J. (1994) 'A licit traffic in cultural objects', paper presented to *Vth Symposium on 'Legal Aspects of International Trade in Art'*, Vienna, 28–30 September 1994.

Meskell, L. (1998) *Archaeology under Fire: Nationalism, Politics, and Heritage in the Eastern Mediterranean and Middle East*. London: Routledge.

Messenger, P. (ed.) (1989) *The Ethics of Collecting Cultural Property: Whose Property?* Albuquerque: University of New Mexico Press.

Micallef, F. and Peirson, G. (1997) 'Financial reporting of cultural, heritage, scientific and community collections', *Australian Accounting Review* 7 (1): 31–50.

Miles, R. and Zavala, L. (eds) (1994) *Towards the Museum of the Future: New European Perspectives*. London: Routledge.

Miller, D., Rowlands, M. and Tilley, C. (eds) (1989) *Domination and Resistance*. One World Archaeology 3. London: Routledge.

Moore, K. (ed.) (1994) *Museum Management*. London: Routledge.

Morris, D. R. (1965) *The Washing of the Spears: A History of the Rise of the Zulu Nation under Shaka and Its Fall in the Zulu War of 1879*. London: Sphere.

National Museum of Denmark (1992) *Sites and Monuments: National Archaeological Records*. Copenhagen: National Museum of Denmark.

O'Keefe, P. J. and Prott, L. V. (1984) *Law and the Cultural Heritage, Volume 1: Discovery and Excavation*. Abingdon: Professional Books.

O'Keefe, P. J. and Prott, L. V. (1992) ' "Cultural heritage" or "cultural property"?' *International Journal of Cultural Property* **2** (1): 307–20.

Orrell, J. and Gurr, A. (1989) 'What the Rose can tell us', *Antiquity* 63: 421–9.

Palmer, N. (1991) 'The law of cultural property and international cultural relations', *World Archaeological Bulletin* 5: 33–41.

Palmer, N. (1992) Editorial. *International Journal of Cultural Property* **1** (1): 5–7.

Pardoe, C. (1992) 'Arches of radii, corridors of power: reflections on current archaeological practice', in B. Attwood and J. Arnold (eds) *Power, Knowledge and Aborigines*. Melbourne: La Trobe University Press, 132–41.

Parker, L. D. (1996) 'Broad scope accountability: the reporting priority', *Australian Accounting Review* **6** (1): 3–15.

Patrik, L. E. (1985) 'Is there an archaeological record?', in M. B. Schiffer (ed.) *Advances in Archaeological Method and Theory* 8. New York: Academic Press, 27–62.

Pearce, S. (ed.) (1991) *Museum Economics and the Community*. New Research in Museum Studies: an international series 2. London: The Athlone Press.

Pearce, S. M. (1992) *Museums, Objects and Collections: A Cultural Study*. Leicester: Leicester University Press.

Pearce, S. M. (1993) 'Museum archaeology', in J. Hunter and I. Ralston (eds) *Archaeological Resource Management in the UK: An Introduction*. Stroud: Sutton, 232–42.

Pearce, S. M. (1995) *On Collecting: An Investigation into Collecting in the European Tradition*. Collecting Cultures. London: Routledge.

Pearson, M. and Sullivan, S. (1995) *Looking after Heritage Places: The Basics of Heritage Planning for Managers, Landowners and Administrators*. Carlton, Victoria: University of Melbourne Press.

Planel, P. (1990) 'New archaeology, new history – when will they meet? Archaeology in English secondary schools', in P. Stone and R. MacKenzie (eds) *The Excluded Past: Archaeology in Education*. London: Routledge, 271–81.

Pokotylo, D. and Guppy, N. (1999) 'Public opinion and archaeological heritage: views from outside the profession', *American Antiquity* **64** (3): 400–16.

Potter, P. B. (1994) *Public Archaeology in Annapolis: A Critical Approach to History in Maryland's Ancient City*. Washington, DC: Smithsonian Institution Press.

Potter, P. B. (1997) 'The archaeological site as an interpretive environment', in J. H. Jameson (ed.) *Presenting Archaeology to the Public: Digging for Truths*. Walnut Creek, CA: Altamira Press, 35–44.

Potter, P. B. and Chabot, N. J. (1997) 'Locating truths on archaeological sites', in J. H. Jameson (ed.) *Presenting Archaeology to the Public: Digging for Truths*. Walnut Creek, CA: Altamira Press, 45–53.

215

Potter, P. B. and Leone, M. P. (1986) 'Liberation not replication: "Archaeology in Annapolis" analyzed', *Journal of the Washington Academy of Sciences* **76** (2): 97–105.

Potter, P. B. and Leone, M. P. (1987) 'Archaeology in public in Annapolis: four seasons, six sites, seven tours, and 32,000 visitors', *American Archaeology* **6** (1): 51–61.

Potter, P. B. and Leone, M. P. (1992) 'Establishing the roots of historical consciousness in modern Annapolis, Maryland', in I. Karp, C. M. Kramer and S. D. Lavine (eds) *Museums and Communities*. Washington, DC: Smithsonian Institution Press.

Power, M. (1996) 'Introduction: from the science of accounts to the accountability of science', in M. Power (ed.) *Accounting and Science: Natural Enquiry and Commercial Reason*. Cambridge: Cambridge University Press, 1–35.

Pryor, F. (1989) 'Look what we've found – a case study in public archaeology', *Antiquity* 63: 51–61.

Pryor, F. (1991) *Flag Fen: Prehistoric Fenland Centre*. London: Batsford.

Pugh-Smith, J. and Samuels, J. (1996) *Archaeology in Law*. London: Sweet and Maxwell.

Quinn, M. (1994) *The Swastika: Constructing the Symbol*. London: Routledge.

Reichstein, C. (1984) 'Federal Republic of Germany', in H. F. Cleere (ed.) *Approaches to the Archaeological Heritage*. Cambridge: Cambridge University Press, 37–47.

Renfrew, C. (1983) 'Divided we stand: aspects of archaeology and information', *American Antiquity* **48** (1): 3–16.

Renfrew, C. (1993) 'Collectors are the real looters', *Archaeology* (May/June 1993), 16.

Renfrew, C. (1995) 'Art fraud: raiders of the lost past', *Journal of Financial Crime* 3 (1): 7–9.

Renfrew, C. (2001) *Loot, Legitimacy and Ownership*. Duckworth Debates in Archaeology. London: Duckworth.

Renfrew, C. and Bahn, P. (2000) *Archaeology: Theories, Methods and Practice*, 3rd edition. London: Thames and Hudson.

Renfrew, C. and Zubrow, E. (eds) (1994) *The Ancient Mind: Elements of Cognitive Archaeology*. Cambridge: Cambridge University Press.

Rentschler, R. and Potter, B. (1996) 'Accountability versus artistic development: the case for non-profit museums and performing arts organisations', *Accounting, Auditing and Accountability Journal* **9** (5): 100–13.

Robins, K. (1991) 'Tradition and translation: national culture in its global context', in J. Corner and S. Harvey (eds) *Enterprise and Heritage: Crosscurrents of National Heritage*. London: Routledge, 21–44.

Sassoon, A. S. (1987) *Women and the State: The Shifting Boundaries of Public and Private*. London: Unwin Hyman.

Schaafsma, C. F. (1989) 'Significant until proven otherwise: problems versus representative samples', in H. F. Cleere (ed.) *Archaeological Heritage Management in the Modern World*. One World Archaeology 9. London: Unwin Hyman, 38–51.

Schadla-Hall, T. (1999) 'Editorial: public archaeology', *European Journal of Archaeology* 2 (2): 147–58.

Schiffer, M. B. (1972) 'Systemic context and archaeological context', *American Antiquity* 37: 156–65.

Schiffer, M. B. (1979) 'Some impacts of cultural resource management on American Archaeology', in J. R. McKinley and R. Jones (ed.) *Archaeological Resource Management in Australia and Oceania*. Wellington, NZ: New Zealand Historic Places Trust, 1–11.

Schiffer, M. B. (1987) *Formation Processes of the Archaeological Record*. Albuquerque: University of New Mexico Press.

Schiffer, M. B. (1988) 'The structure of archaeological theory', *American Antiquity* 53 (3): 461–85.

Schiffer, M. B. and Gumerman, G. J. (eds) (1977) *Conservation Archaeology: A Handbook for Cultural Resource Management Studies*. Studies in Archaeology. New York: Academic Press.

Scott, D. D., Fox, R. A., Connor, M. A. and Harmon, D. (1989) *Archaeological Perspectives on the Battle of the Little Big Horn*, Norman and London: University of Oklahoma Press.

Scovill, D. H., Gordon, G. J. and Anderson, K. (1977) 'Guidelines for the preparation of statements of environmental impact on archaeological resources', in M. B. Schiffer and G. J. Gumerman (eds) *Conservation Archaeology: A Handbook for Cultural Resource Management Studies*. Studies in Archaeology. New York: Academic Press, 43–62.

Shanks, M. (1992) *Experiencing the Past: On the Character of Archaeology*. London: Routledge.

Shanks, M. and Tilley, C. (1987) *Reconstructing Archaeology: Theory and Practice*. Cambridge: Cambridge University Press.

Skeates, R. (2000) *Debating the Archaeological Heritage*. London: Duckworth.

Smith, L. (1993) 'Towards a theoretical framework for archaeological heritage management', *Archaeological Review from Cambridge* 12 (1): 55–75.

Smith, L. (1994) 'Heritage management as postprocesual archaeology?' *Antiquity* 68: 300–9.

Smith, L. (1995) 'Cultural heritage management and feminist expression in Australian archaeology', *Norwegian Archaeological Review* 28 (1): 55–63.

Smith, L. (1996) 'Significance concepts in Australian management archaeology', in A. Clark and L. Smith (eds) *Issues in Management Archaeology*. St. Lucia, Qld: Tempus Publications, University of Queensland, 67–77.

Smith, L. (2000) ' "Doing Archaeology": cultural heritage management and its role in identifying the link between archaeological practice and theory', *International Journal of Heritage Studies* 6 (4): 309–16.

Smith, L. and Campbell, G. (1998) 'Governing material culture', in B. Hindess and M. Dean (eds) *Governing Australia*. Cambridge: Cambridge University Press.

Smith, L. and Clarke, A. (eds) (1996) *Issues in Management Archaeology*. St Lucia, Qld, Anthropology Museum University of Queensland (= *Tempus: Archaeology and Material Culture Studies in Anthropology* 5).

Somerset County and District Councils (1989) *Protecting the Historic and Architectural Heritage of Somerset*, written by R. Lillford and R. Croft. Taunton: County and District Councils of Somerset.

Stanton, P. and Stanton, J. (1998) 'The questionable economics of government accounting', *Accounting, Auditing and Accountability Journal* **11** (2): 191–203.

Startin, B. (1993) 'Assessment of field remains', in J. Hunter and I. Ralston (eds) *Archaeological Resource Management in the UK: An Introduction*. Stroud: Sutton, 184-96.

Stone, P. and MacKenzie, R. (eds) (1990) *The Excluded Past: Archaeology in Education*. London: Routledge.

Stone, P. and Molyneaux, B. L. (eds) (1994) *The Presented Past: Heritage, Museums and Education*. London: Routledge.

Sullivan, S. and Bowdler, S. (1984) *Site Surveys and Significance Assessments in Australian Archaeology*. Canberra: The Australian National University Department of Prehistory Research, School of Pacific Studies.

Swanson, J. A. (1992) *The Public and the Private in Aristotle's Political Philosophy*. Ithaca, NY, and London: Cornell University Press.

Swidler, N., Dongoske, K. E., Anyon, R. and Downer, A. S. (eds) (1997) *Native Americans and Archaeologists: Stepping Stones to Common Ground*. Walnut Creek, CA: Altamira Press.

Szacka, B. (1972) 'Two kinds of past-time orientation', *Polish Sociological Bulletin* 1–2: 63–75.

Tainter, J. A. and Lucas, J. G. (1983) 'Epistemology of the significance concept', *American Antiquity* 48: 707–19.

Tarlow, S. (1999) 'Wormie clay and blessed sleep: death and disgust in later historic Britain', in S. Tarlow and S. West (eds) *The Familiar Past? Archaeologies of Later Historical Britain*. London: Routledge, 183–98.

Thoden van Velzen, D. (1996) 'The world of Tuscan tomb robbers: living with the local community and the ancestors', *International Journal of Cultural Property* 5 (1): 111–26.

Thomas, J. (1991) 'Reading the body: beaker funerary practice in Britain', in P. Garwood, R. Skeates and J. Toms (eds) *Sacred and Profane: Proceedings of a Conference in Archaeology, Ritual and Religion*. Oxford: University Committee for Archaeology, 33–42.

Thomas, J. (1993) 'The politics of vision and the archaeologies of landscape', in B. Bender (ed.) *Landscape – Politics and Perspectives*. Oxford: Berg, 19–48.

Thomson, J. (1977) [1877] *Public and Private Life of Animals*. London: Paddington Press.

Thompson, M. (1979) *Rubbish Theory: The Creation and Destruction of Value.* Oxford: Clarendon.

Thornes, R. and Bold, J. (eds) (1998) *Documenting the Cultural Heritage.* Los Angeles: J. Paul Getty Trust.

Tilley, C. (1989a) 'Excavation as theatre', *Antiquity* 63: 275–80.

Tilley, C. (1989b) 'Interpreting material culture', in I. Hodder (ed.) *The Meanings of Things: Material Culture and Symbolic Expression.* One World Archaeology 6. London: Unwin Hyman, 185–94.

Tilley, C. (1994) *A Phenomenology of Landscape.* London: Berg.

Tillotson, R. G. (1977) *Museum Security/La Securité dans les musées,* ed. D. D. Menkes, trans. Marthe de Moltke. Paris: ICOM.

Trigger, B. G. (1984) 'Alternative archaeologies: nationalist, colonialist, imperialist', *Man* 19: 355–70.

Trotzig, G. (1987) 'Some thoughts on the archaeological heritage', in *Archaeology and Planning: Architectural Heritage Reports and Studies 5.* Strasbourg: Council of Europe, 2–7.

Trotzig, G. (1993) 'The new European Convention on the protection of the archaeological heritage', *Antiquity* 67: 414–15.

Tunbridge, J. E. and Ashworth, G. J. (1996) *Dissonant Heritage: The Management of the Past as a Resource in Conflict.* London: John Wiley and Sons.

Turkel, G. (1992) *Dividing Public and Private: Law, Politics, and Social Theory.* Westport, CO: Praeger.

Tzanidaki, J. D. (2000) 'Rome, Maastricht and Amsterdam: the common European heritage', *Archaeological Dialogues* 7 (1): 20–33.

US Department of the Interior (1989–90) *Federal Historic Preservation Laws.* ed. S. K. Blumenthal. Washington, DC: US Department of the Interior.

Uzzell, D. (ed.) (1989a) *Heritage Interpretation: Volume 1. The Natural and Built Environment.* London: Belhaven Press.

Uzzell, D. (ed.) (1989b) *Heritage Interpretation: Volume 2. The Visitor Experience.* London: Belhaven Press.

Uzzell, D. (1989c) 'The hot interpretation of war and conflict', in D. Uzzell (ed.) *Heritage Interpretation: Volume 1. The Natural and Built Environment.* London: Belhaven Press, 33–47.

Uzzell, D. (1998) 'Heritage that hurts: interpretation in a postmodern world', in D. Uzzell and R. Ballantyne (eds) *Contemporary Issues in Heritage and Environmental Interpretation: Problems and Prospects.* London: The Stationery Office, 152–71.

Van Zyl Slabbert, F. (1992) *The Quest for Democracy: South Africa in Transition.* London: Penguin.

Van Vuuren, D. J., *et al.* (eds) (1991) *South Africa in the Nineties.* Pretoria: HSRC.

Wainwright, G. (1989a) 'The management of the English landscape', in H. F. Cleere (ed.) *Archaeological Heritage Management in the Modern World.* One World Archaeology 9. London: Unwin Hyman, 164–70.

Wainwright, G. (1989b) 'Saving the *Rose*', *Antiquity* 63: 430–5.

Walsh, K. (1992) *The Representation of the Past: Museums and Heritage in the Post-modern world*. The Heritage: Care, Preservation, Management. London: Routledge.

Walsh, K. (1995) 'A sense of place: a role for cognitive mapping in the "postmodern" world?', in I. Hodder, M. Shanks, A. Alexandri, V. Buchli, J. Carman, J. Last, and G. Lucas (eds) *Interpreting Archaeology: Finding Meaning in the Past*. London: Routledge, 131–8.

Way, T. (1997) 'The victim or the crime: park focused conflict in Cambridge-shire and Huntingdonshire 1220–1556' in J. Carman (ed.) *Material Harm: Archaeological Studies of War and Violence*. Glasgow: Cruithne Press, 143–66.

Wenban-Smith, F. (1995) 'Square pegs in round holes: problems in managing the Palaeolithic heritage', in M. A. Cooper, A. Firth, J. Carman and D. Wheatley (eds) *Managing Archaeology*. TAG. London: Routledge, 146–62.

Wester, K. W. (1990) 'The current state of cultural resource management in the United States', in B. W. Andah (ed.) *Cultural Resource Management: An African Dimension*. Forum on Cultural Resource Management at the conference in honour of Professor Thurstan Shaw. *West African Journal of Archaeology* 20: 80–8.

White, H. (1973) *Metahistory*. Baltimore: Johns Hopkins University Press.

Williamson, T. and Bellamy, L. (1987) *Property and Landscape: A Social History of Land Ownership and the English Countryside*. London: George Philip.

Wilson, P. J. (1988) *The Domestication of the Human Species*. New Haven and London: Yale University Press.

Wilson, D. (1989) *The British Museum: Purpose and Politics*. London: British Museum Press.

Woods, D. (2000) *Rainbow Nation Redeemed*. London: André Deutsch.

World Archaeological Bulletin 6 (1992) Special issue on the Reburial Issue. Southampton: World Archaeological Congress.

Wright, P. (1985) *On Living in an Old Country*. London: Verso.

Yates, T. (1988) 'Michael Schiffer and processualism with a capitalist S', *Archaeological Review from Cambridge* 7 (2): 235–8.

Yoffee, N. and Sherratt, A. (eds) (1993) *Archaeological Theory: Who Sets the Agenda?* New Directions in Archaeology. Cambridge: Cambridge University Press.

Young, L. (1994) 'Significance, connoisseurship and facilitation: new techniques for assessing museum acquisitions', *Museum Management and Curatorship* 13: 191–9.

Zimmerman, L. J. (1989a) 'Made radical by my own', in R. Layton (ed.) *Conflict in the Archaeology of Living Traditions*. London: Routledge, 60–7.

Zimmerman, L. J. (1989b) 'Human bones as symbols of power: aboriginal American belief systems toward bones and "grave-robbing" archaeologists', in R. Layton (ed.) *Conflict in the Archaeology of Living Traditions*. London: Routledge, 211–16.

Index